UNFINISHED BUSINESS

Unfinished Business

Leon Yoder

Sycamore Systems Inc

Middlebury IN

CONTENTS

ACKNOWLEDGEMENTS

To acknowledge everyone that was influential in the content of this book is not feasible, but greatly appreciated nevertheless.

This project would not be without SuEllen, my wife, and wonderful partner that has inspired and supported me through all my entrepreneurial seizures over the years!

Thank you, Dave Kauffman, for all the opportunities and for telling me to write this book. The love and support of my business associates, the Phenomenal Five. My brothers, Al, Norm & O.W., for the inspiration to always stretch a little further. My Dad for his extreme patience in teaching us the trades.

To all my employees over the years, you taught me many things I wish I could have learned quicker, but cherish the relationships.

To my spiritual mentors, Terrill & Todd, that changed the trajectory of my life. Dustan, for your friendship and valued perspective.

With love to my wonderful children, Cherith, Grace, Corban, Esther, and Carson!

PREFACE

Solomon said that there is nothing new under the sun, yet each of our lives is a unique creation made up of all these elements that are not original with us but are compiled in a way that never was before or will be again.

The thoughts and ideas in this book are a compilation of my thoughts and experiences that I hope might be an inspiration for someone else. These ideas are not intended to be comprehensive and cover every perspective, but rather inspire the questions that generate great conversations and moments of learning for the readers. It's difficult to learn when you don't know the right questions to ask. I hope this inspires the right questions.

Though the satisfaction is great in finishing what became a passion for me, this writing also makes me keenly aware of my many failures over time. Seldom, if ever, do we make an original mistake so hopefully, this will enable you to skip a few that I already made.

With Best Regards, Leon Yoder

CHAPTER 1

THE BEGINNINGS OF A BUSINESS

 *atthew 6:33 But seek first the kingdom of God and His righteousness, and all these things shall be added to you. NKJV*

At the core of the American dream is this concept of owning a small business, this great entrepreneurial endeavor that lured us in with the promise of freedom in both finances and time, this hollow promise that was supposed to set us free from the chains of employment and provide us with more time and money to spend on our families.

Many of us found quite the opposite. We took the job we loved and became a slave to it. The work that was supposed to set us free became our master. We are having to work so many hours that our work is now just a job that we own.

So how did this happen?

Many small businesses are started by craftsmen or skilled technicians who are excellent at their trade. They see an opportunity in their market, a need that is not being filled, and embark on this entrepreneurial voyage to fill this gap.

At first, it's great. The market doesn't change much and the competition stays the same. The business begins to grow and maybe even adds a few employees. But inevitably the market shifts, the competition changes, and suddenly, we realize we can't do business like we have always done business.

Our business has grown bigger than we planned. We're producing more products or services than ever before and have some employees, yet there seems to be less profit than when we first started. What about all this paperwork and taxes? I don't recall signing up for this!

In the eyes of our friends and neighbors, we have achieved the American dream. We are now a small business owner, and yet, we feel like the business now owns us! We sense that a change has taken place. If we are to survive as a business, we will need to make a change. We have to quit the job we had within our own business and switch from being the craftsman or technician to a business manager and leader.

I experienced this very same thing when I first started a business. I reached a point where I had to decide if I was going to remain the sole designer and salesperson in my graphics company or step into a management role. It wasn't until a few years later after taking that step that I was challenged by a business coach with the concept of "finishing your business". Of course, this sounds pretty strange to any business owner because we all recognize that any business requires continuous development and is never really finished. However, this phrase is about developing your business to the point that you can either sell the business or choose what level you want to stay involved and have it continue to operate without relying on you for the day-to-day operations.

Many small businesses are started but left unfinished.

SELF EMPLOYMENT, A JOB THAT YOU OWN

I do want to make a disclaimer. There are small businesses where the owner of the company is also one of the main workers and may even have an employee or two and is able to be very successful. Everyone involved makes a good living, and they will even occasionally have to turn away work because they are not able to provide service to everyone that comes along, but the business does well. A business is successful if it provides the livelihood the owner desires or needs. The tricky part is knowing what you are willing to settle for in wants or needs.

This can be a successful model if it is properly planned for. But it also has its own set of challenges. It is in many ways a job that you own. If you, the owner, do not show up for work, you basically won't get paid. In other words, if you stop, the business stops. If it's a service-oriented business and a client has an emergency, it will probably be you that has to make that evening or weekend service call.

The key to making this model a success is recognizing that you will have to place a limit on what you can offer and how many clients you can serve. This means you will need to be more selective in the clients that you accept because you realize you can't serve everyone that comes along and therefore will need to select those that are most profitable for your specific business model.

It can be very tempting to try and take a large job that is bigger than what is suitable for you because it looks like good consistent money for an extended period of time, but it will also tie up all your resources, and you may need to hire additional help to complete the job on schedule. This is a growth trap that many small businesses will readily walk into if they have no plan.

You have to be prepared to turn down some jobs like

this because they don't fit your model. In turn, you might be able to be a fill-in and be a subcontractor for a larger company (which you may see as your competition at times) that does take this job and is better equipped for this scale of job. You have to be okay with knowing that not every job is a good fit for you, especially in this 1-3 person small business model.

The surest way to not get anywhere is to not define a destination.

BUT IF YOU'RE NOT GROWING YOU'RE DYING

Many Christian businessmen have fallen into a trap because of this motto that the business world has declared. Yes, it is true that if you are not growing you may be losing, but only as long as we properly understand growth.

Some think that growth is always in size. To keep growing, we have to keep growing bigger and adding more employees and try to enlarge our share of the market. Now, I understand the human reasoning behind this, but from a Christian perspective, this in itself is simply greed.

I had a client tell me of an instance where a fellow Christian turned down a simple cross-marketing opportunity that would have been great for both of them simply because the one was afraid the other might make a dollar off of him. That's correct, not that he would lose a dollar, but he simply didn't want the other to make money off of his business. Needless to say, the one who declined is no longer in business.

I have also seen in the same Christian community a very successful businessman helping someone else start the same kind of business that he, himself, had because he could no longer supply the market, and rather than grow larger, he helped a fellow Christian start his own small business. Now that does require a lot of respect and integrity in both parties to work together in such a manner knowing you could ultimately become competitors.

But regardless of our viewpoint, it is simply bad business to think that growth is only in market share. True growth is the process of continuous development rather than just building a bigger building or producing more product.

Growing in efficiency should be one of our highest priorities. There are some amazing examples of what companies have done with efficiency growth in itself. There are numerous concepts such as Lean, Six Sigma, and Scrum or Agile Project Management that are dedicated to higher efficiency. Higher efficiency results in lower stress in the workplace which is often a safer workplace.

The growth of a business is ultimately anything that improves its ability to better achieve the owner's life goals. Growth might be increasing the profitability by a smaller number of jobs but choosing better jobs. It may be dropping a less profitable product line to enable expanding another. It might mean less overall profitability for the owner because he is putting more of the profits toward the employees to ensure they remain engaged in the business and in return giving more freedom to him as the owner. Growth can come in many shapes, forms and methods.

So whether you want to remain a 1-3 person business where you remain as one of the primary employees or technicians, or you want to grow a self-sustaining business that can continue without your day-to-day involvement, many of these same concepts will apply to either model. The focus, however, of this book is toward the business owner who wants to implement systems and procedures that will provide more freedom and enjoyment in managing and growing their own company.

When people start a small business they usually have a plan of some sort.

I realize some really don't have much of a plan other than "we're going to build this new gizmo and sell them like crazy". This kind of business usually lasts no longer than their plan. Once the "crazy" ends, the business ends.

I know some very successful businesses have been started with a simple plan written on the back of a napkin. It doesn't have to be elaborate or very extensive to be a good plan. But you do need a plan.

We often envision a business plan as this thick stack of paper with endless numbers, background details and elaborate descriptions written in "lawyerese" that is for the sole purpose of impressing your banker enough to give you the capital you need to start your business. A formal business plan is certainly appropriate for large startups, but our focus here is a leaner working plan to help get you on track.

A common business plan would start with a summary and include sections covering the company, product or services offered, market research and feasibility, the strategy, goals and milestones, operations including employees and management team and, of course, the financials, budget and sales projections.

An even more basic business plan should at least cover these fundamentals: Feasibility, Strategy, Operations and Numbers, and we'll replace the standard summary with an even shorter version we will refer to as an "elevator pitch". This basic Four Dimensional Business Plan will be what we focus on here. But before we start, let's begin with one question.

WHY?

Why do you want to start your own business?

Many small businesses are started with too many misconceptions and end in disappointment. So to spare you some grief, let's look at a few possible reasons.

I can't stand working for my boss. He's impossible!

I understand. I had the same boss once, but there are a few things to keep in mind. Once you become your own boss, you might find that he, too, can be pretty difficult at times.

Secondly, imagine that boss being your customer. Yes, that's right, and you will be needing a lot of customers.

I want to make a lot more money.

There are many versions of this, but they all encompass the idea of being financially independent and that small business owners all make the big money. True, there are small businesses that do very well financially. But those profits are not the result of casual 8-5 workdays. It is extremely hard work that for the most part will not feel like it is worth the trouble.

In our local area here in northern Indiana, this is especially true. We have many RV and related manufacturing jobs that pay a very lucrative wage with no upfront investment. The most common misconception is that a small business owner will make more money than a factory job.

If this is your only motivation, I would advise you to save yourself the headache, invest wisely and enjoy the time with your family.

I want to have more free time.

As the saying goes, "when you start your own business,

you only have to work half days, and you can decide which 12 hours you want to work". Of course, if there is no one to cover the holiday or someone is sick, or quits, or needs to stay late, yes, it usually will be up to you to cover. You are the last to leave and the last to get paid.

Now, if you still have any inclination to start your own business after that reality check, then you just might have what it takes to be an entrepreneur.

Truly, there are also some benefits to being a business owner and, actually, the whole point of this book is to help you eliminate some of the general pitfalls.

NO, IT'S NOT ALL BAD

Yes, you will have many more bosses than you have ever had. But customers can also be a huge blessing, too. I have established many great relationships through my small business.

Yes, there will be long hours, and to start out, you might wish you only had to work 12 hour days, but if you have a proper plan, you should be able to delegate a lot of the work as you progress and build your company. You can only work those long hours for a certain length of time before you will get burned out or sick.

Yes, it may take a couple of years for you to match what you are currently making on your day job, but once a business is established and a team in place, a small business, with the proper systems in place, can provide you with more flexibility and an operation that will continue even on your day off.

Yes, you may have to fill in for the guy that quits, meet that customer after hours and fix something on the weekend, but you will also, eventually, be able to take a few days off. Maybe even a week for vacation. Plus, you can take your vacation at a different time than everyone else.

Ziglar small business coach, Howard Partridge, said there is only 1 reason for your business to exist.

"Its only purpose is to help you achieve your life goals". Period.

It can be a rough vehicle at times, but it can be an effective vehicle. It drives best, however, when you understand the why.

MAKE A PLAN – THE PITCH

A standard business plan usually begins with an executive summary. For our basic Four Dimensional plan, we will trade our summary for an elevator pitch. An elevator pitch is exactly that – a summary or pitch that you can share with someone in about the same amount of time as an elevator ride.

An elevator pitch is generally used in regards to sales and in selling your products or services. But for right now, there are no products or services unless you can convincingly sell your family, your banker or investor and even yourself on this great business idea.

Imagine you step into an elevator with Warren Buffett (considered by some to be one of the most successful business investors in the world, worth over $72 Billion in 2017) and he asks you if you know of a business he could invest in. You have about 30 seconds.

Do you try to cover everything you can in those 30 seconds? No, because he would probably think he got hit by a verbal tornado. What you would want to do is tweak his interest enough in 15 to 30 seconds that he would be interested enough to schedule a meeting with you to look at your full business plan.

It is much like fishing. You prepare the bait and dangle it very carefully knowing you are not given much time to hook the fish. The hook is merely the means of bringing it to a point where the deal can then be landed properly.

This may sound manipulative, but it should not be. It is more about being tactful, about being respectful of others who may not be as enthused about the opportunities that excite you.. But dangling choice pieces of the information allows them to decide if they are interested in your venture or not.

Now the chances of you running into Mr. Buffett might be a little slim, but this same pitch will be very useful in convincing your spouse, family or some other business partner that this is an idea worth pursuing.

So to get started, you might want to jot down your initial idea or rough pitch first and then jump into developing the four elements of our basic plan.

FEASIBILITY

This first step is the big qualifier. If these questions can be answered convincingly enough, it might actually be worth going through the next three steps.

Is there an open need for the product or service you want to provide?

By open, I mean, is there an available share of the market open? If you are simply producing the same thing someone else is and simply plan to sell it for a dollar less so that you can try to take their market share, then I would suggest you keep your day job because it is simply a race to the bottom.

If you have no niche other than price, you generally do not have a sustainable business plan. Granted, there are models or companies that focus on having the lowest price, such as a WalMart or Dollar General store. Even these companies have an elaborate marketing plan to back that "lowest dollar" image. Inevitably, someone else will come along and try to build your same product for a dollar less than you. Sometimes, they might simply be aiming at a larger market and intend to lower production costs with higher volume. Even if they are losing money because they didn't do their proper homework, they may not run out of money before you do.

You might say this is crazy. Nobody actually starts a business this way. I would agree if I had not seen it happen as many times that I did.

Fred sees his neighbor Joe starting to build gizmos, and after a year or so, Joe has added on to his building. He has a couple of employees and seems to be doing pretty well.

Fred says, hey, I can build gizmos just as good as Joe can and maybe even better than him. I will start building these part time after work and make a little extra money.

Fred has no real overhead costs because he does not have to pay any insurance and payroll taxes, and he is simply doing it in his garage or his basement, so the extra money looks pretty good. Plus, he doesn't have a problem selling them because he is selling them for five dollars less than Joe.

Orders start picking up a bit for Fred and he has to work quite a few hours to keep up, and he still has his regular day job because there is not quite enough profit to do it full time but almost too much work to just do it part-time.

In addition to this, Fred realizes that if he is going to do it full time he needs to have more room. Now if this would happen to be the same way that Joe started and Joe was doing it for five dollars less than Sam, who was doing it before Joe, then Fred might be getting to the point where he will have a tough time being profitable, not to mention Sam and Joe who have had to both cut their prices to be competitive with Fred.

Unless the market demand for gizmos has drastically increased, these guys will be chasing each other to the bottom until someone drowns.

So back to the beginning. Unless you can design and build a better gizmo or else the market is so large that the demand is not being met, you need to consider how feasible or even ethical it is for you to start producing them.

Maybe there is new technology that allows you to produce them much more efficiently than what is currently being used for production. There are instances where companies get comfortable with absolutely no competition and are selling an overpriced product. This may open opportunities in the market for a midrange gizmo that another group of people would buy if available.

The important thing is to properly analyze the cost of building these as if you were doing it full time and paying yourself like you would have to pay an employee.

Is it sustainable? If not, then you are only ruining the market for someone else who is trying to make a living and provide for their family.

THE COUNSEL OF OTHERS

Proverbs 15:22 Without counsel plans fail, but with many advisers *they succeed. ESV*

Do not overlook seeking the counsel of others. It is not only good practice, it is also biblical.

Do you have a good enough understanding of the field you are entering? Have you solicited the input of an industry insider to look at your plan?

If you are married, have you sought advice from other self-employed family men to gain an understanding of how this might affect your family? Most important of all, is your spouse fully on board with your plan?

Generally, the spouse will place security over adventure

or risk. We all have various gifts and strengths, but I have personally found my wife to be my greatest sounding board. If I cannot convince her, it usually is not a very good plan. But most importantly, you both need to be in agreement with the plan.

Your accountant or tax professional as well as your banker and local advertising agent are great people to seek counsel from because they have an understanding of the local economy and maybe even of your specific industry.

Last but definitely not least is your pastor or spiritual advisor. This person will be looking out for your spiritual well-being and believe me, starting a small business can take a toll on a person spiritually. You will want that groundwork solid.

Some Additional Questions

Do you have the means or facility to produce this product? Do you have sufficient financing to provide those means or facility?

What are the price points for this product or service? Is there enough margin to sustain growth?

What is the competition? What is their market share?

This leads us to the strategy.

STRATEGY

How do you plan to sell your product or service? Is it a wholesale product or sold through distributors? Is it a business-to-business service or retail?

Who exactly will buy this product or service? What is the potential market? Have you defined your demographics properly? How will you market this, and what are those costs? Do you need a salesperson?

How long will it take to implement the marketing and start producing sales? Do you have sufficient finances to sustain this startup period? Is your location suitable? This is extremely important for a retail business.

Do you have realistic goals and milestones set?

Do you have a contingency plan if you do not hit those goals? In other words, do you have the finances to survive the inconsistencies in the cash flow?

A very helpful tool to analyze and build your company strategy is to do a SWOT (Strengths, Weaknesses, Opportunities, Threats) assessment. Following is a copy of the assessment I developed for our clients.

This assessment is aimed at existing businesses but is equally helpful to startups, though some of the questions might not be as pertinent to a new business.

STRENGTHS, WEAKNESSES, OPPORTUNITIES & THREATS (SWOT) ANALYSIS

Strengths:

1. Why should I buy your product or services? vs competition

    1. What do you do really well?
    2. What sets you apart?

2. What advantage does your company have in this marketplace?

    1. Special equipment, staff, location, technique or procedure, financial.

3. What part of your business is the most profitable?

    1. Why is it the most profitable?

Weaknesses:

1. In what areas are you least equipped or lack resources for this market? (staff, equipment, location, finances, systems)

   1. Should you avoid certain areas?

2. What's the first improvement you would like to see?
3. What is the least profitable aspect of your business?
4. What might be the biggest risks involved in this venture?

Opportunities:

1. What are areas of the market currently underserved?

   1. What needs or niche are your competitors missing?

2. Is there new technology, equipment, new processes or intellect that could leverage new advantages in the market?
3. Are there any new trends in the marketplace?

   1. Have the needs of the clients changed?

Threats:

1. Who are your primary competitors?

   1. What is their primary strength?

2. Are there secondary or potential future competitors that could affect your market?
3. Are there market changes happening?

4. What effect might economic conditions have on your plan?
5. Are there government regulations?
6. Does your company have any specific vulnerabilities?

    1. Financial liabilities?

OPERATIONS

What facility will it require? If you hit your projections, what will it require in two years? Five years?

Do you need a retail location? Do you have the proper location? There is an old saying regarding a retail business, but it merits being said again, "the three most important things in retail are location, location, and location".

I recall a situation where a client of ours had built a brand new store, much larger than the original building and only a few hundred feet from the original store. They continued to use the original store for their one department that they wanted to expand. We created large new signs, and they added some features to draw people into the original store, but even though it was in the same parking lot, they later made the comment that it might as well have been two miles away. They removed the building and added to their existing store to accommodate that department, and it is one of the most successful stores around.

What kind of equipment will you need? What kind of staff will you need?

How long will it take to set up and be open for business?

NUMBERS

Do you have an accountant? An accountant can help assist you in setting up a proper accounting system.

Do you have sufficient capital for the startup? Can you sustain the initial marketing and launch phase? Can you absorb the uneven cash flow that might occur at times?

What are your overhead costs? These costs, your rent, utilities, phone, advertising, etc., are not billable. They will be due each month whether you produce anything or not.

What are your operating costs? These are the weekly costs of staff, materials and such that are directly involved in either the production of the product or service you provide and will fluctuate with the volume produced.

A plan doesn't have to be fancy, but it has to be as real and as straight to the point as you can get it. The more questions you can answer now, the better chance you have of succeeding.

DON'T WRITE IT IN STONE

The only thing more important than having a plan is to be willing to change it.

Pro boxer Mike Tyson said, "Everyone has a plan 'till they get punched in the mouth."

In the 20 years I had a sign shop and was working with new businesses, I do not recall ever seeing a startup that had a specific plan for their product or service that they were going to provide without having to change anything in their plan after a year or two.

As the ancient philosopher, Heraclitus wrote, "There is nothing so constant as change."

There will always be new competition, new technology and changing trends in the market.

Remember that your product is not your child, and sometimes, you have to discard it for another.

In the 20 years, I was in the sign business, the industry dramatically changed. It went from hand-painted signs to digital prints. Certain products were selling for less than when we had started.

People tend to lament the changes and only see the disappearing opportunities, but I believe that for every opportunity lost there are 2 new ones.

I remember when the Walmarts of the world, the big box stores, started moving into areas and taking their toll on the downtown shops. That small Mom and Pop grocery store had to close because they could not compete with the big chain store. But I imagine that there was a time when the butcher and the baker may have been put out of business by that grocery store. Now just recently, we started seeing those big chain stores closing the doors because of the internet and big online retailers like Amazon.

So has the market come full circle in the last 100 years? Today because of the Internet, individual craftsmen are able to market their handmade products to the whole world.

There is a friend of ours that has a flourishing business selling the products they are building at home on Etsy. Etsy is currently one of the largest online markets for handcrafted items. We visited a young couple in another state, and the wife had converted the basement area into a little shop area where with the help of a few neighbor girls she was producing products that she was selling on

Etsy. There are amazing opportunities for craftsmen that did not exist just a few years ago. The local cobbler that was run out of business a long time ago has a market again, the world wide web. His workshop is at home, and his storefront reaches across the whole world.

Many of the downtown areas of cities and towns are reinventing themselves with coffee shops and restaurants and providing almost park-like gathering areas for people to hang out. People have a strong need to connect with others and are drawn to gathering places.

When Jesus was teaching about the cost of discipleship, he said this in Luke 9:62-

"No one, having put his hand to the plow, and looking back, is fit for the kingdom of God."

This same advice is profitable in the market. It is difficult to stay on course when you are constantly looking back. It is good to know who your competition is, but don't get sidetracked with trying to put them out of business. Focus on being a leader in the market and let them try to chase you.

CHAPTER 2

A FOUR DIMENSIONAL BUSINESS MODEL

L *uke 14:28 For which of you, intending to build a tower, does not sit down first and count the cost, whether he has enough to finish it. (NKJV)*

I developed the following Four Dimensional Business Model to illustrate the basic components of a small business and its functions in Fig. 2-1.

The Central Gear is in the center of the model and contains the four basic elements of a business.

Finances. Every startup business will require some startup capital. This amount is crucial. You can have a successful startup, but if you don't have sufficient finances to absorb the initial cash flow cycles or the additional growth spurts, insufficient operating capital can close down the most successful operation. It is not unusual to hear startups say they should have had about twice the startup capital than they had planned for.

Product. Even if you offer only services, your services become your product. Anything you are selling to your clients becomes your product.

Sales. Of course, without sales, your venture is only a hobby and not a business.

People. Your business begins and ends with people.

If you do not have all four of these elements, you do not have a business.

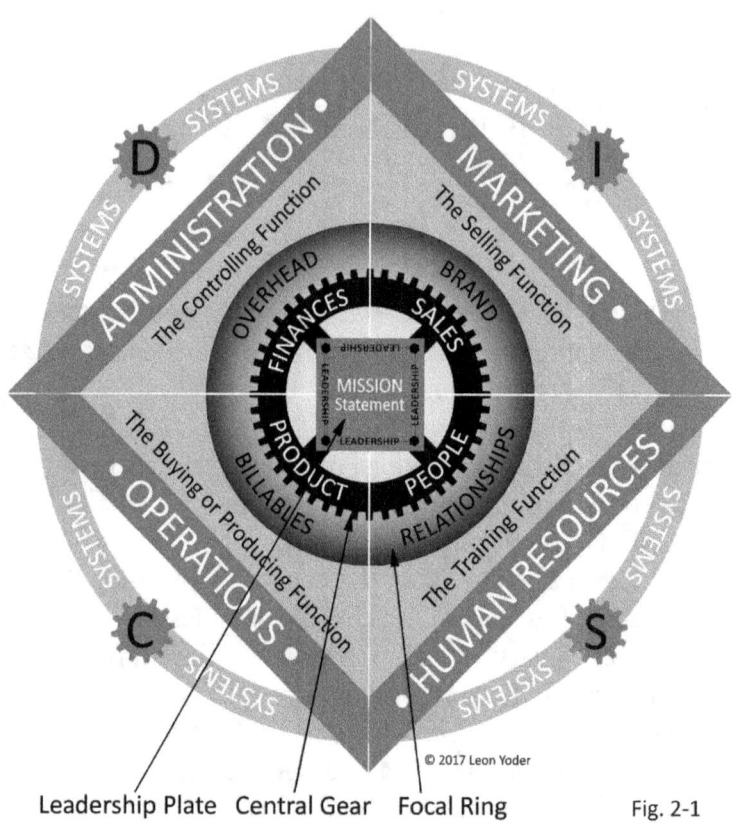

Leadership Plate   Central Gear   Focal Ring   Fig. 2-1

The Leadership Plate is at the very center and is what holds the Central Gear together. At the very center of this leadership plate is the company's mission statement. A good mission statement should be central to all of the leadership's decisions. Too often even if there is a mission statement, it is a lengthy statement that no one remembers and is located in the outer corners somewhere. This statement should give basic direction and vision for the company, starting with leadership.

The Focal Ring is the circle surrounding this Central Gear. These four elements, Overhead, Brand, Relationships, and Billables are key to keeping a company healthy. As important as they are, they are easy to lose focus of in the busyness of business.

The Circle of Systems encompasses the whole model, all four business segments, and is really the key to completing your business. Witten systems or Standard Operating Procedures (SOPs) are the keys to operating a business successfully and consistently without being enslaved to the business. These SOPs are crucial to defining and holding quality standards, properly training employees and are sometimes helpful in holding over-ambitious business owners to specific procedures that have been agreed upon.

The DISC Personality Gears within the Circle of Systems are there to remind us of the various personalities that make up our organization. This is an element that if properly understood and utilized will become a crucial component in how well your organization functions.

THE FOUR BUSINESS SEGMENTS

So, why the four segments? Why have a model like this?

It's like the old question, how do you eat an elephant? One piece at a time. Likewise, any large project is better managed when it is broken down into smaller segments where it can be properly measured and managed. Dividing a business into these four function-based segments allows one to focus in on a smaller portion of the company. These four segments are universal across all kinds of small companies rather than looking at the business on a department level. The different departments in a company can vary greatly depending on the type of business.

Later as we get into developing systems or procedures and training tools, it becomes much easier to focus on one segment at a time.

While business models can become very complex, and dividing them into four basic sections makes them easier to remember, each segment may still contain many individual departments and functions that can become quite complex.

Administration. The administration segment can be seen as the Controlling Function of the business. This segment is a two-edged sword. Certain business owners, depending on their personality and management style, will tend to enlarge this segment beyond what it should be, losing focus of the overhead that it is creating. Others will see administration only as overhead and will tend to not have enough administration in place to operate smoothly. It is important to always keep the overhead in focus as this is a recurring cost of doing business.

Marketing. The need for sales is quite obvious. Sales are at the very core of the marketing effort and are usually treated as a separate department from Marketing. But, it is all part of the selling function. Marketing has to do with identifying the potential clients for your product and then developing a strategy for exposing your product to them. *Advertising* is the promoting of that product or service with a strong call to action in the message to encourage or initiate the purchase. *Sales* is the process of actually selling that product or service. *Branding* is another function of the marketing segment of a business. A brand is a term, design or image that helps identify and differentiate your product from your competition. It reinforces what your product is all about. Branding has to be consistent throughout all of the marketing efforts. It is important to not lose focus on the brand when developing new ads and marketing plans.

Human Resources. The human resources are the most valuable resources a company has. Every business starts with a person and their vision. The ability to grow a business will be in direct relation to how well you can train and develop the people involved. The health of the company usually depends on the health of relationships within the organization.

Operations. Every business has to have a product. If it is a service-oriented company, then the service is the product. The product is whatever it is that you sell. Operations cover the complete process of developing a product or service through the production and delivery of that product. Sometimes when a company is in a stage of retooling or reorganizing to streamline the operations, it is important to not lose focus on the billable hours or products that are being produced. When the amount of billables goes down, so does the company cash flow.

DEVELOPING A MISSION STATEMENT

Many business owners will agree that developing a mission statement is very important to a business. Yet, many business owners never seem to find the time to create one.

So, what is a Mission Statement, and what should it accomplish for a business?

A mission statement is made up of various elements that are easier to understand if it is broken apart and the elements developed separately. The elements are the mission, vision, purpose and core values of a company. We will look at each one individually.

The mission statement is the primary statement that defines who you are to your clients. Some of the other elements may be included in this statement but in its most basic form should explain why you exist, what you provide and for whom. It should define who you are to your clients and provide direction and inspiration for both your leadership and employees.

Following are a few examples of mission statements.

Google To organize the world's information and make it universally accessible and useful.

Coca-Cola To refresh the world... To inspire moments of optimism and happiness... To create value and make a difference.

Toyota To attract and attain customers with high-valued products and services and the most satisfying ownership experience in America.

General Electric Invent the next industrial era, to build, move, power and cure the world.

Facebook Give people the power to share and make the world more open and connected.

Nike To bring inspiration and innovation to every athlete* in the world. *"If you have a body, you are an athlete." – Bill Bowerman

Wal-Mart Save people money so they can live better.

I always think of a vision statement as stating what we want to be when we grow up. This should reflect the company's ambitions. Such as "To Be The Best 'Product or Service' In The World", or "Have Our Product In Every Household In America". The vision should be a dream that is big enough but also real enough that it will inspire your people. It sets the picture of what the future success of the company looks like.

The purpose statement is the "why" behind what you do. Often, the core values are incorporated into this statement as well.

Having a separate core values statement can be a powerful tool to keep an organization on track, especially for nonprofits and organizations that may receive community support and, therefore, need to uphold high values in their operation. A values statement will also be helpful in maintaining a company culture and work environment.

PEER POINT

David Kauffman - Empowering Small Business, Sarasota, FL

A Mission Statement is what you do today to serve your clients. It's YOUR mission–good leaders judge by mission and not by emotion. So your Mission Statement should be clear, concise, and hard-hitting. It should do three things: It should inspire your clients, it should guide your employees and it should govern your business decisions inside your business. For example, my company's mission statement is TO HELP BUSINESS OWNERS FIND FREEDOM IN THEIR BUSINESS, SO THEY CAN SPEND MORE TIME WITH THEIR FAMILY AND FRIENDS.

You also need to communicate to yourself, your employees and your customers your vision. Actually, the mission statement is the vision statement in action. It's like telling people where you're headed... This is where this company is going. You wouldn't want to get on a plane if you didn't know where it was going—right? Well, neither do employees. When you're clear on where your plane is going, then people who want to go there will want onboard and that translates into people who want to work with you. They're the ones who will be committed to helping you get there. For example, our vision statement is TO BE A HOUSEHOLD NAME GLOBALLY IN THE BUSINESS WORLD. Everyone in our company lines up with that.

A purpose statement is WHY you do what you do. A greater moral, social, value. Your purpose should be something larger than just producing what you produce or what your business does. You have to identify what that is... your purpose is what fuels the airplane and keeps everything going. Your company's purpose is your internal compass. It keeps you on track. Our purpose statement is TO COACH, TRAIN AND MOTIVATE BUSINESS OWNERS TO THE LEVEL OF SIGNIFICANCE.

When you are ready to create your Mission, Vision, and Purpose (MVP) statement. It can be a great exercise to get everyone in your company involved. Depending on the size of your company, you may want to break up into groups of three or four to do the initial brainstorming.

Some questions that can spur some ideas for the initial brainstorming:

Why does our company exist?

What area or whom do we serve?

What do we do best, and why is that so great?

What effect or impact do our services or products have on people?

Assemble these ideas and sort and note the best answers and start putting these together in statements and keep combining, condensing and simplifying until you think you have a pretty good summary. When you think you are done, post it somewhere for a few days and then try editing it again. Can it be shortened or said in a brighter, more powerful way?

Some will say your mission statement should be one sentence, others a few paragraphs. I discovered that the shorter the statement, the more powerful and effective it is.

Avoid using empty buzzwords or phrases that could apply to many different companies.

It should define who you are and be meaningful enough that it sets the direction for every decision that is made in your company.

Ideally, it will affect or be relevant to both your clients and employees as well as you, the owner.

The mission statement should be as short and concise as absolutely possible.

I remember when we were working on the mission statement for our sign shop, Legendary Designs, Inc., and I had just put the final touches on our statement when a business associate called me. I was quite pleased with our three-paragraph statement until I read it aloud to my associate. Suddenly, it didn't sound near as good as I thought it was.

It seems there is always a shorter, more concise way to say something. The better you can summarize something, the better you can define it.

After quite a bit more work we had reduced it to 3 sentences. This made it much more memorable and meaningful.

The first sentence was the mission statement oriented toward our clients "Provide effective signs and graphics that build a legendary identity for our clients."

The second sentence was posted in the shop and reflected our vision and how we could know if we were successful or not. "Our Success Is Defined By How Well

We Accomplish The Goals Of Our Clients and Affect Our Community."

Our third sentence was about our purpose. "We exist to help every employee in achieving their life goals and ultimately to further God's kingdom."

Our core values were included in both our vision and purpose.

This was the result of an original statement that consisted of three lengthy paragraphs and slowly condensed in stages. The more condensed it became, the more meaningful and powerful it became.

DIFFERENT VALUES FOR A CHRISTIAN?

As a Christian business owner, we do have some things to consider in establishing our core values that other business owners may not. Though most any business owner will see the value in having honesty and integrity as part of their core values, they may not feel obligated to some of the other biblical principles that a New Testament Christian will find important.

This subject of how these Christian principles are applied in business is well covered in the book by Gary Miller, titled, It's Not Your Business. Miller examines some of the ideas that seem to contradict Jesus' New Testament principles with those in the Old Testament book of Proverbs.

Ultimately, there will be differences between a business based on kingdom principles and one based only on profit.

If our business plan is based on kingdom principles, the core values and our plan for growth will be directed by what we believe God has called us to do. Growth in profits may be seen as a means to expand a ministry rather than personal wealth. Expansion possibilities will be evaluated by how it will affect our personal and family life and not just by potential profits.

These are things that each Christian has to search out and apply as convicted.

NAMING YOUR BUSINESS

Naming your business is such an important decision in the development of your business, and yet, you usually only have to make this decision once. It is difficult to get good at something you only do once.

Naming your business is like laying the foundation for a building. Once it is done, it is difficult to change or correct. If something is off, it only becomes more obvious as you build on it. The only thing worse than not having a name that works well is not being willing to change it.

NAMING GUIDELINES

Avoid misspelled or hard to pronounce names. Think about answering the phone every two minutes and having to say your business name each time. Is it too long or too difficult to pronounce? Do you have to spell it each time someone asks for your business name to ensure that it is spelled correctly?

Your name should reflect the values of your company. It needs to resonate with who your company is. In the brainstorming sessions, think of the benefits your company provides and not necessarily the products. Incorporating a product word into your name is not wise because eventually the market may change, and you may either add or change what products you provide.

The tendency is to get everyone involved in the naming process, the family, friends, employees, clients etc. This may be helpful at times, but this can turn into a stressful matter because of people's egos and feelings, and you end up trying to appease people rather than selecting what really is best for the company. So, be careful in selecting your committee. A good place to look for some professional help on this would be the graphics design company you plan to use to develop your logo and additional branding and advertising materials.

One of the most qualifying factors in selecting a name is, of course, whether it is original or different enough to stand out from the competition. Is the name available as a domain name? You always want to reserve the internet domain name for your company if at all possible. The .com domain is most desirable for commercial companies. Sometimes, .net is preferred by tech and internet-based companies. The .org domain is generally used for non-profits and various organizations. The .biz and .us domains are also becoming more common for companies as the .com's become unavailable. Sometimes when the specific domain isn't available, you can use a phrase such as BackyardPondPro.com or MyNewCar.com. Using a keyword or product word can be useful for search engine optimization (SEO) purposes.

NAMING TECHNIQUES

There are many different naming techniques for naming your company and some good reasons not to use certain ones of them, and yet, there can be exceptions to probably everyone.

I have observed that certain techniques seem to trend, such as #3 below. Many companies in the early 20th century simply used the founder's name, sometimes the full name such as Walt Disney, Charles Schwab or Wm. Wrigley Jr. Co. Sometimes, they used the first initials and last name, or, in case of partnerships, both last names. For example, H.J. Heinz, Studebaker, Harley Davidson.

Another very common use was the combination of #2 and #3, such as Ford Motor Co., Turner Broadcasting, and Kraft Foods.

Concerning trends in names, it seems that when companies become very successful, their naming technique will be duplicated by other new companies. In the late '90's there were many companies using the .com with their name until the end of the dot-com boom. Currently, in my area in Northern Indiana, there is a trend of utilizing initials along with industry or product name. This works fairly well up to point until, given the number of small businesses in our area, it becomes harder and harder to build a unique brand or identity using that same naming mechanism. Following are the names of six different woodworking companies I found listed in our area with these very similar names: L&L Woodworking, L&M Woodworking, L&N Woodworking, L&R Woodworking, L.A.M.B. Woodworking and L R M Woodworking. This adds an additional challenge when trying to develop a unique brand or image with this.

Some of the following naming techniques are definitely better than others, but none of them are absolutely wrong. It is a matter of what works best for your company image and what will set you apart in your field. Much of it depends on if a certain technique gets overused in an area.

1. Locations. Many companies use a city, state, county or some other name relating to their location as part of the company name along with a reference to their product or industry. This worked great for Minnesota Manufacturing and

Mining company until they started growing beyond their state and specific industry. This innovative company is now nationally known as 3M. Kentucky Fried Chicken rebranded as KFC to deemphasize the regional identity. Keep in mind that your products and the market area may change over time.

2. Product or industry names. Many times it may not be the best idea to use a specific product name because of the potential changes in the market and the focus of your company. With that said, there are times when it does work well because the name describes what you do, for instance, Brownsville Carpet Cleaning. You immediately know where they are located and what they do. The problem happens when they expand and start covering other cities as well as add other services such as pressure washing. Suddenly, the name is not broad enough..

3. Name and initials. This was used extensively in the late 19th and through the 20th century for companies such as J.P. Morgan, L.L. Bean, H.J. Heinz, Levi Strauss, Sears, Roebuck, and Co. Some large companies have used initials only to abbreviate longer names such as CVS (Consumer Value Stores), BMW (Bavarian Motor Works), UPS (United Parcel Service). This initials-only concept can work for large established companies but is generally not as effective for a startup. Also, it is difficult to find an available domain for short abbreviations like this. One of the major drawbacks of using your personal name for your small business is that, if you ever want to sell your business, the new owner may

not want to use your personal name. It may not
be an issue if your business is built into a major
brand.
4. Geographical feature plus industry name. This is
   another mechanism that sees a lot of use in my
   local area among small businesses, and it works
   fairly well for woodworking and trades-oriented
   businesses and farms until, like any naming
   technique, it gets overused and they start
   blending together. Some geographic examples
   are Riverside RV, Woodside Taxidermy, Hilltop
   Machine, Southedge Furniture, Streamside
   Wood Shop, River Woodworking.

Other variations of the geographical elements that are
used by a couple of local restaurants are 41 Degrees
North and one that uses actual directions from the primary stoplight in town, West On Warren.

1. Common or Cliche names. I would recommend
   avoiding the more common terms even though
   we have companies like General Electric,
   General Motors, American Specialties, etc. Using
   common names such as General, American,
   Custom, Country or ending with Enterprises,
   Specialties, etc. will require a lot of marketing
   efforts to develop a brand. Some of the cliche
   terms that depict being the best in the field can
   work if they are not overused within a specific
   market. Terms like Superior, Quality, Ultimate,
   Elite, Legendary, Peak, Summit etc.
2. Misspelled or created words. This is generally
   not the best practice because it usually creates
   names that are difficult to spell and pronounce.
   These become very tempting, especially when

trying to find an available domain name. Some successful examples include Xerox, Verizon, Spotify, Etsy, Microsoft. Keep in mind what the marketing budget is for these companies. Some of the partial words that are commonly used in combination with others are Quali-, -tech, -tronix, -matic, -soft, -aton and -co. Many companies have simply added -co to the end of initials or a name such as Geico, Jayco, Rayco etc. Generally, you should avoid misspelled words. They are difficult to find in an online search or any directory listing.

3. Compound Words. This is a technique that is being used a lot in the tech world and enables you to create an almost endless variety of unique names by combining two words into a unique compound word. Some successful examples are Facebook, Firefox, Photobucket, JotSpot, WordPress, YouTube, Salesforce.

4. Descriptive Word Combinations. This is a slight variation of #7. This is the combination of a descriptive word plus an object. The descriptive word might be a color or element combined with person, place or thing. Examples are Purple Cow, Tin Monkey, Red Bull, Black Anvil, Iron Mountain.

5. Mainstream Words. This simply uses one mainstream word, and although it might limit the potential variety of names, it does hold some great potential for names. A few well-known examples are Target, Gap, Staples, Apple.

6. Industry Jargon. Many names utilize words, a play on words or names of items from the specific industry such as Cinnamon Stick,

Kitchen Cupboard, Red Wagon. Hair salons often use a play on words such as Shear Delight, A Cut Above, etc.

What will they call it?

Sometimes we come up with a great name. We have a logo, signs and all the promotional work done, and then you begin to hear people call it anything but the name you gave it. I've learned the hard way that if a name is slightly awkward to say, people probably are not going to use it. Maybe the name is too long or simply doesn't fit the location. If this is the case, they will abbreviate it or use a version that feels comfortable.

I handled the marketing for an event center that was named the Michiana Event Center, but we tried to brand it as "the MEC". This was a case where the name may have been too short because what we most often heard was "MEC Center". Whatever the case may have been, "MEC Center" felt phonetically more comfortable to most people.

In another case, we had a local client that built a large, beautiful multi-tenant wood post-frame building in the style of an original Amish farm barn. The exterior was the traditional barn red. This business was named Yoder's Dutch Country Store. We built large attractive signs for each side of the building that were easily readable from any angle plus an additional sign out beside the road. But it didn't matter how nice the name was or how beautiful the signs were because the facility itself carried a major presence, and everyone, locals and visitors alike, kept calling it either "The Big Red Barn" or "Yoder's Red Barn". I can still see Bob, the owner, come into the shop about a year later shaking his head, " I guess we'll change the name to what everyone calls it, Yoder's Red Barn."

DEVELOPING A LOGO

The first thing after a business name is established, a logo should be developed. A well-developed logo will add an established feel to your new business as well as reinforce the overall image of the business.

This will build customer confidence. They can see that you have put thought and planning into your business and expect that to carry through to your product.

Look at your logo in black and white before you settle on the design because some designers will try to embellish it with fades and colors that seem attractive at first but won't appear as attractive once it is reproduced in a black and white ad or an embroidered logo on a shirt.

The simpler the design, the better it will reproduce on smaller promotional products.

DEFINING A LOGO & DIGITAL ARTWORK

The term logo is the most common term used to relate to what can be either a logomark, a logotype, or the combination of both.

logomark	logotype	combination mark

 **Adobe**

Once you settle on the design of your logo, you should make sure the designer provides you with digital files in multiple file formats and both in black and white and in color. You should request the files in both bitmap and vector formats. See the following diagram that illustrates the difference between bitmap and vector. In a bitmap image, the graphic or photo is made up of tiny pixels with each pixel having its own color. A vector file is a graphic made up of individual nodes with a straight or arcing line connecting each node to create a specific shape that will then have either a solid color fill or may be filled with a gradient color. These individual shapes then make up the complete image. Vector files are used for CNC routing and vinyl cutters and are also modified to be used to create embroidery. Vector images can be scaled to any size and never lose quality in the resolution.

Most general bitmap formats are .jpg .tiff and .png files. A .png is quite useful because it is a bitmap that can have a transparent background around the graphic. This is useful for web and other printed graphic designs.

The common vector formats are .ai for Adobe Illustrator or .eps. Both of these file types are usually provided to your print shop or graphic designer. A vector .dxf file is usually used for producing work on a CNC router or laser.

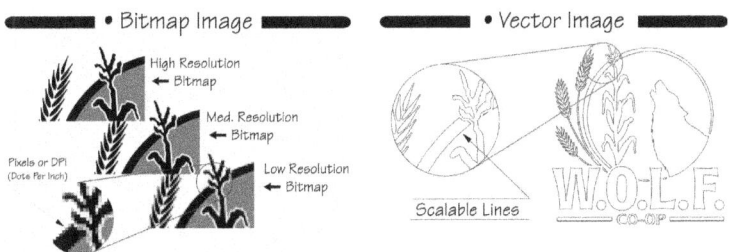

Along with the logo, the colors and supporting artwork should be kept consistent across all of the advertising, website, signs and marketing materials to promote and reinforce your brand. Your brand will generally be your client's first impression of your company. You only get one first impression.

CHAPTER 3

SYSTEMS, THE POWER OF PROCESS

---

*P*roverbs 16:3 *"Commit to the Lord whatever you do, and he will establish your plans."* *(ESV)*

System [sis-tuh m] 1. an assemblage or combination of things or parts forming a complex or unitary whole: a railroad system. 2. a coordinated body of methods or an orderly plan or manner of procedure; an organizational scheme: a system of government.

The more I set up and use systems within my business, the more I become aware of the systems around me. It is easy to see that our creator God is a God of order. There is an order and a system to everything he has created, from the tiniest seed growing into a large tree, the whole ecosystem of a forest and how it takes care of itself. Especially after a seemingly devastating forest fire, we see how it is designed to recover and even some of the benefits that it gains from that fire. It is an incredible system, and it is only one of the countless systems that are around us. From the structure of our DNA to the massive expanse of our solar system, we see the evidence of design and order, the fingerprint of God in everything he has touched.

At first, it might seem that a system is restrictive, that it would hinder our freedom. But the reality is that there is great freedom within a system because it does restrict us from doing things that are not beneficial and helps us to easily repeat what we have found to be good. Not only does this system allow us to repeat our successes, but it allows us to duplicate that success in others.

Reflecting back to when I was a young man working in a tool and die shop, I recall when I first learned how to read blueprints. Those blueprints were very detailed, providing all the specifications required to build the various products that we produced. I remember how those blueprints opened up a whole new world of possibilities to me.

I discovered that the true power of a blueprint lay in the ability to define tolerance in a dimension.

An example would be a plate of steel that needed 2 holes, each one 1/4" in diameter, and the center of the holes was to be 3" apart. If those holes were drilled with a 1/4" drill bit and had to match another set of holes on a machine that this plate was bolted to, and those holes were exactly 1/4" and I was using a 1/4" bolt, it was very likely not going to fit unless both holes were machined with extreme precision. There was simply no tolerance figured into the dimensions to compensate for the slightest variation.

To machine, both pieces with that much precision on a piece that did not require that kind of accuracy would have only created a lot of manufacturing cost for no good reason.

So drilling both of those holes with a larger 5/16" bit and defining a tolerance of +/- 1/16" on the 3" dimension would allow enough variation to produce the piece in a cost-effective manner and still provides assurance that the 1/4″ bolts were going to fit when assembled.

This is what makes a blueprint work properly. The specified tolerance sets a benchmark for what is acceptable and what isn't. This allows a part to be built efficiently within a reasonable range of accuracy.

This gives the design engineer the control he needs to have over the production of the parts to ensure that all the parts will fit and his completed machine will work as he intended.

Blueprints For Business

Some years later when a business coach first introduced me to systems for managing a business, I recognized that having written systems are like having blueprints for running your business. Systems or Standard Operating Procedures (SOPs), which is what they are usually called, define in simple steps how something should be done. I'll be referring to these simply as systems.

Now a lot of things don't have to always be done precisely the same way, but if the proper tolerance range and quality standard are specified, the owner can expect the job to be completed correctly.

THE START TO COMPLETING OUR BUSINESS

I was the owner of a sign shop when I was first introduced to systems. The sign shop consisted of two employees and me at the time, and I was really intrigued by the concept but almost immediately did what every other business owner does. I went into denial, and yes, I said the same thing everyone else says.

"My business is different. It wouldn't work in this business"

As I pondered the possibilities of systems and how it

could apply to my business, I wasn't convinced that it could be done with what we were doing.

In our business every single job was different.

First, even the applications were usually different. It could be vinyl lettering applied to a vehicle or a sign of about any size using a wide variety of materials. It might be a billboard size advertising sign or a small interior directional sign. On top of everything else, I was personally designing each job, and we had at this point established a reputation for a certain "look"? How was I going to put that into a system that someone else could duplicate?

Well, as they say, desperate times call for desperate measures, and one day as I was talking to a local business coach, I again made my case that too much of our business required me to have my hands on each of the projects or at least the larger projects.

I remember well when he just looked at me and said somewhat crassly, "you're not **#*%* Van Gogh. You can train someone else to design your signs just as well as you."

Now, I did know who Van Gogh was, and I certainly didn't see myself in that category, but I was hit with his bluntness. I couldn't help but keep pondering this.

So what if he was right? Could it be done? What would that look like?

One thing I concluded was that if I could make systems work for this business, systems could work for any business out there. Surely this had to be one of the hardest kinds of businesses to develop systems for. Hardly anything we did was the same. Every sign was custom designed and each one built differently.

I think the challenge itself enticed me as much as realizing what the benefits might be.

THE FIRST STEPS

I took the biggest challenge first-the pricing.

I had to do almost all the pricing because with every project being different it was anything but an exact science.

It was difficult enough for me to price these jobs much less to train an employee to do it and come up with the same pricing.

I did have a printed pricing guide that was published by a trade magazine and using this as a basis, I started developing a spreadsheet. I kept developing it in stages and testing it until I had a concept that I thought would work.

For about a month I would go back to work after the family went to bed and would work on spreadsheet formulas until I fell asleep. After sleeping for a couple hours, I would work on it some more and then go home in time for breakfast and another nap before it was back to work. I did this multiple times a week for a month until I had it completed.

We started testing it. I would give the specifications for a sign or vehicle lettering to the secretary and we would both enter it and after some tweaking of the spreadsheet we were consistently coming up with the same price.

Here again, it was a matter of tolerance. It wasn't going to be as exact as quoting out each sign piece by piece, but it was much faster and consistent enough to make up for any dollar or two that we might miss on the occasional quote.

Once this pricing system was developed and implemented, I began to see the tremendous potential of systematizing more things. Even if I couldn't create a system for the designing, it wouldn't matter if I could get everything else.

We kept developing systems, and I had started delegating some of the simpler design work to the secretary, things like vehicle numbers and some of the simpler layouts. She had no formal training in design work before this, and as I kept giving her pointers on how to tweak the designs, I suddenly discovered she was doing layouts that looked a lot like what I would have done. She was picking up my design style simply by watching what I produced.

I began to see the possibilities of delegating more of my design work.

Soon after this, we hired another designer, a young guy who had taken some schooling in graphic design and had a clear desire to learn. I had him sit in on some of my design sessions, and I would describe out loud why I was doing things in a certain way as I worked on the design. I was surprised at how much of my design work had very logical steps to it. I could explain how I arrived at a certain point.

I so clearly remember the day that I walked into the shop and saw a design that he had done for a personal project for one of the employees, and I stopped in my tracks. It was a unique design, but it looked exactly like something I would have designed. It had the same look and same feel. It was an empowering moment.

After 19-1/2 years we sold the sign shop to a local printer that was expanding their operations. Even though we were still working on developing systems and did not have things perfected, we did have enough systems in place that I was able to step back from the day to day operations and was only at the shop about half a day per week for the last year or so of owning it.

One of the last systems we developed involved our bonus system for employee payroll. This system was crucial in getting the employees engaged on another level.

The last year I owned the business I was paying them higher wages than I ever had and yet was still making a consistent profit. The profit margin was not huge, but it was more consistent and with much less involvement from me than at any other time in the 19 years before that.

I will cover this incentive-based pay system later under the Team Building section.

DESIGNING A FASTER FOOD SERVICE

I was working with a local event center where we had installed a new kitchen, and a few members of the management team spent a lot of time developing a way to produce the burgers fast enough during our larger events. After some trial and error, they figured out how to prepare enough burgers in the time frame needed without assembling them too much in advance to still preserve the freshness in the bun, etc. There were other processes as well that needed to be developed, such as how to produce enough fries at the right time and keep them fresh and crisp enough when they were ordered.

These were all systems or procedures that were developed to ensure that enough food could be produced fast enough to serve a large amount of people in a short period of time. This worked well for a year or two. But as our events kept getting larger, our problem kept getting bigger as well.

During a specific event that had grown exceptionally, large we had food lines that stretched halfway through the building, and people had to wait up to an hour to get their food. We had three large windows that we served through, and we were as efficient as any fast food restaurant, but it simply wasn't good enough.

This can become one of the most challenging situations

for a business. You've worked hard to develop a system that works smoothly and efficiently until you've increased volume or experienced enough other changes that you run into a situation where a system that worked just fine suddenly is drastically insufficient for what you need.

Loving a challenge, I offered to try and find a solution. I was familiar with the concept of lean manufacturing but was by no means an expert on it. Our solution came out of these principles.

LEAN PRODUCTION & SIX SIGMA

Lean production involves continuous efforts to eliminate or reduce 'muda' (Japanese for waste or any activity that consumes resources without adding value) in design, manufacturing, distribution, and customer service processes. Lean is very structured in its approach and keeps value to the customer as one of the highest goals. Lean relies heavily on the complete involvement and empowerment of every team member.

At the end of World War II, W. Edwards Deming, an American engineer, and consultant gave numerous lectures in Japan helping their industry leaders develop better quality control systems and better management practices that the U.S. industry leaders had rejected. The U.S. was the leader in the global industry, and many industry leaders saw no need for any changes.

Toyota Motor Corporation developed these ideas into what we now know of as Lean Manufacturing or Just-In-Time (JIT) process. The Toyota Production System (TPS) had such an impact on the quality and efficiency of their product that finally the U.S. automakers had to take notice and eventually asked Deming to help them implement some of these same systems.

With the TPS Lean concept, any problems in the quality are quickly identified early in the process so as to eliminate large runs of defective items. It also required a mindset of constant improvement, of continually looking to remove wasted or non-value added movements within production.

Six Sigma is a process developed by Motorola in 1986 and is a strategy to improve the quality of products or services produced through the removal of defects and errors until It is expected to be statistically free from defects. Elements of this process are often incorporated into lean principles.

There are numerous books written about each of these processes, and I do not intend to elaborate much on either one of these other than to note the role that they play in relation to systems as they are tightly integrated. These two processes are two of the most commonly used tools and concepts that are being used today to improve the systems or procedures within a business.

Back to our problem at hand that required a faster food service. This is a good example of how you sometimes have to totally reinvent a system to produce the desired results. To get started, I tried to totally discard the thoughts of how we were currently doing it. I began analyzing it from the opposite direction, beginning from the customer's standpoint and not the production point. Walking through these steps, I envisioned coming up to the food window and imagining how could I get what I needed with the absolute shortest number of steps.

Eventually, I came up with a completely different approach where I didn't place an order but rather picked up the sandwich I wanted from a row of slides with heat lamps similar to what you see in fast food restaurants that are between the kitchen and the server. Here the client became the server himself. The kitchen staff could monitor the slides and keep a number of sandwiches on the slide. Drinks and fries were served in a similar manner, only the drinks were obviously placed on a flat slide area. So we would have to use up most of the areas of two of our serving windows for this process.

We still had a problem. People would still require a certain amount of time to make payment. So the facility manager developed the idea of setting up a separate table situated away from the serving windows where we could set up multiple registers to take their payments.

Then came the part that can be the most challenging at times, which is to get the manager and all the employees to buy into this idea of a totally new process without making anyone feel like they were not doing a good enough of a job and without making them feel we were running over them. This can be a delicate situation at times, and it is so important to get everyone's input because they also hold the capability of making sure it doesn't work if wrong attitudes are created. But, of course, our manager and employees were of the highest character and put all their effort into trying it even though a few may have been slightly skeptical.

The results were incredible. It actually worked almost better than I had imagined. We created only one line up to the food, and at the busiest times, people could still move through the line in about 5 minutes.

It did create a few more issues in the kitchen where they had to slightly modify the processes for a few things, but those were worked through fairly swiftly. With the same amount of staff, we drastically increased the number of people we could feed.

Many companies have had major improvements in their production to square foot ratio through implementing lean manufacturing principles. Regardless of what we are doing, there exists the possibility of improving the process.

Kaizen is the core of lean manufacturing, believing that the possibility of improvement always exists.

The amount of improvement that can be made will continually be smaller as the improvements are implemented, and at some point, the improvements may not be big enough to justify the effort it takes to find them. We often think we have arrived at this point long before we actually do.

I have also encountered people that have had bad experiences with lean because the principles were improperly implemented, and it didn't result in any improved efficiencies but only bad attitudes. It's not only important to have a proper understanding of the principles that are being applied but also to have your people on board with the ideas and understand them enough to believe in them.

If you can't describe what you are doing as a process, you don't know what you're doing. *Edwards Deming*

DEFINING A SYSTEM FOR SYSTEMS

So what does this look like when a company has systems?

In reality, every company already has systems for everything. The problem is that each employee has a system of how they do their job. It just isn't documented, and it may not really be the right way to do it.

So that greatly diminishes the possibility that the company has actual control over the quality of what is being produced, and even if it is done correctly, there is no sure way to guarantee the process will be duplicated or repeated.

So for systems to do the liberating work that they

should, they need to be documented and usable for both reference and future training purposes.

The following is one way of documenting those systems or Standard Operating Procedures (SOPs) as they are usually called.

You create a 3 ring folder for each of the four different segments detailed in chapter two. Create an index page with a tab for each department or key function within that business segment. In the folder for Administration, you might have an index and tab for Office IT (Information Technology). This index page would list the name of every task or process related to the Office IT. A corresponding page number would follow each task. An item is added to the index list each time a new process is added to that section in the folder. Some processes or tasks might be easily explained on one page and others might take a number of pages, but the index will simplify finding the specific task or process.

To document a new process, you start with a new page that has the title of the process at the top of the page. A few of the things that might be included at the beginning of every process might be what resources are needed to complete the process, how often or what determines when the process is to be done and, maybe most importantly, the standards that have to be met. This will define whether or not the process has been completed properly. The technician has to know when it is done.

How to write the actual steps to the process can vary quite a bit depending on the complexity of the task or process.

Sometimes a simple list of steps will be sufficient. Often times a flowchart showing each step in a more visual manner can be much easier to follow than a numbered list. If it is a process using software, the steps might include a screenshot for each step showing how each step is completed. If it is a maintenance process, it might show a picture that was taken of the inside of a piece of equipment and have a few arrows to show where to grease it.

Sometimes a short video clip becomes the easiest way to show a short and quick process. This is not a problem if your 3 ring binder is actually a digital document and you can embed the video directly into the page. However, this won't work as well if you are using real paper. One of the solutions to this is to upload your video clip to your public folder in Dropbox or pCloud online service and then copy the link to that video and search the web for a QR code generator and convert your link into a QR code that you can insert into the process. Now, whether you use a digital version or a paper version, you have the link available to either click on in the digital copy and a QR code that an employee can scan with their smartphone and connect to that same video with just a simple click.

These processes can be easily created using MS Word or any other document editor, including some online editors such as Google Docs, which can be used when the documents need to be shared with other team members. Most of these editors will have the ability to insert screenshots, smart objects such as flowcharts, photos, videos etc. If you create a separate document for each key function or section using an editor like MS Word, you can create a self-generating index on the first page by using a Heading format for each new process title you add.

Flowcharts are very useful to show the flow of a process, especially in instances where decisions have to be made within the process that will affect what steps are taken in relation to that decision. Fig. 3.1 shows some of the various shapes that can be used in creating a flowchart. The diagram in Fig. 3.2 shows a sample of a regular flowchart and how these symbols might be used in documenting a process in your business.

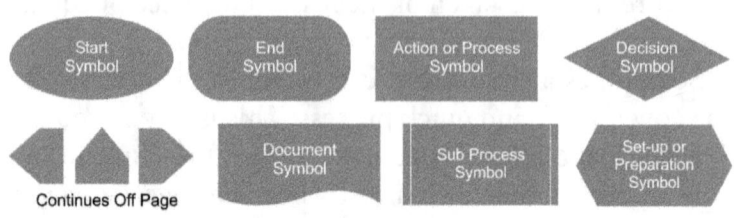

Fig. 3.1

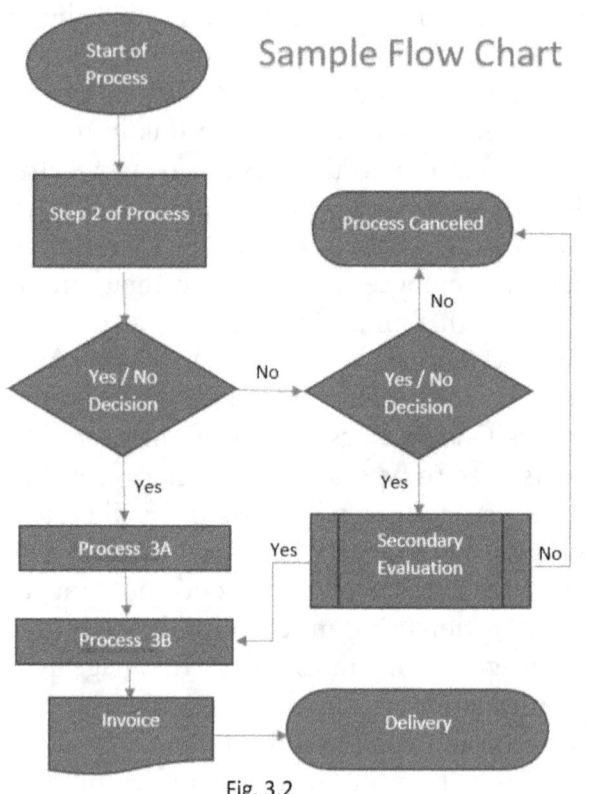

Fig. 3.2

FROM THEORY TO APPLICATION

So, you create a manual of Standard Operating Procedures and document every process in your business from opening up the doors in the morning to closing up in the evening, and your work is done and you live happily ever after. If only it was that easy!

No, not all the challenges are eliminated by creating these procedures. It is no doubt a tremendous tool, and I could ramble on about all the advantages you can experience when you have these processes documented. But instead, let's look at some of the associated challenges.

Developing systems is a process itself that is never completely done. Even before you have everything documented that you would like to have, you will need to review some of the existing ones and probably streamline and improve some of the existing processes. You should always be seeking to improve the processes.

So how does one know where to start and stop?

One of the first steps, especially if you are a "C" type personality in the DISC Model of Human Behavior, is that you will need to remember that there are real people involved in performing these processes. It is extremely important to bring your complete team on board with these changes as they are implemented. Otherwise, you will see a lot of uncooperative attitudes develop if you try to implement these principles on your own. It has to be a team effort.

Whenever management starts looking over an employee's shoulder to try an analyze the steps of everything they are doing, it will make them feel like management thinks that they are not doing their job. This will cause resentment and spell failure before you even start.

TWO LEVELS OF SYSTEMS

I prefer to define systems into two levels. The first and primary level is systems that show the overall process or flow of a key function in your business, for example, a flowchart showing the process for hiring and training new team members or a process that shows the complete sales funnel from how a lead is managed through processing the order. It might be a process of how these procedures will be managed and maintained because there is work involved in maintaining and updating these operating procedures. This primary level covers the flow or process of how each department operates.

The secondary level of systems is focused on the more detailed tasks within each department or key function. Where the primary system might show the overall computer network in an office, the secondary system might detail the steps to installing the printer software on a single workstation.

It usually makes the most sense to start by identifying and documenting the primary systems within a company. This establishes an overall framework of the company and documents how the primary information flows through the company. This can include the management structure and set the standards for scanning files and how they are labeled. This might seem like a small thing until a company has three to five years of data that is spread throughout multiple computers and storage drives and is filed in so many different ways that it all becomes useless because it simply becomes cost prohibitive to reorganize it and to rename files so that they can even be effectively searched.

After the primary systems are established, then it is easier to focus on documenting some of the secondary, more detailed procedures.

It usually makes the most sense to start with problem areas, areas in the operations that are producing mistakes or inconsistencies. Have your team members help analyze the whole process. Have it be their problem and, even

more importantly, their solution. It is of utmost importance that they not only feel that they are part of the team
but that they actually have to work as a team with each
individual having a say in the process, where each idea is
noted and evaluated by every other one no matter who
provides it. Your best ideas will come from the people
who are most directly involved in the process. As solutions are developed and documented, they'll begin to see
the benefits of these operating procedures. It establishes
a standard that everyone can rely on. It ensures that efficiencies can be easily repeated and with less stress.

Another area that is pretty easy to start with is any
procedure that is only done occasionally such as certain
maintenance items. These are processes that are often
overlooked unless you already have a dedicated maintenance person in place. Something such as checking all fire
extinguishers and testing exit lights could be recorded as
a process and a checklist created that has to be checked
and signed off by whoever is appointed to do this. Most
team members will see the simple value in this, and it is an
easy way to begin to implement systems into the workplace. Once people see how these checklists and processes
are helping to eliminate some of the mistakes and are
actually making their work easier, it becomes much easier
to have everyone on board with documenting procedures
and to keep developing new ones and improving old ones.

WHEN SYSTEMS FAIL

There are numerous reasons that systems fail or at least
appear to fail.

First of all, you need to know that some team members,
also formerly known as employees, will resist systems
because systems hold people accountable. Occasionally,
you will have people who do not want to be accountable,

and those are usually the very ones who need it most. You may find it will eventually weed out some members who don't fit well on the team and having them leave may be better in the long term for both you and the team.

When you first introduce systems to your team and are preparing to implement them in your company, it is important that the team members feel like they are receiving additional tools that will make their jobs easier and less stressful. Systems are sometimes seen as just another protocol to follow, just another tool that is only useful from the management's point of view and will only add extra responsibility and workload onto the rest of the people. It is better to expect it to be a hard sell and be pleasantly surprised rather than expecting everyone to immediately catch on to the vision and then be discouraged when it doesn't happen.

PEOPLE ABOVE PROCESS

Another problem has to do with flexibility in the systems. You can have issues in both extremes, being too rigid and also not being rigid enough. You always need to place people above the process.

These processes are not the US Constitution. It should not take an act of Congress to change them. But in the same instance, neither should they be able to be changed without proper approval and evaluation.

When you have one group working in harmony with a system and another part of the team is totally disregarding the process, you will have chaos on top of chaos and bad attitudes within the mix. You have to hold that balance where everyone abides by the processes, but once it becomes obvious that the process is broken, repairs need to be made quickly. As beneficial as systems can be, a broken system can cause damage quickly. Proper systems will increase efficiencies and reduce stress, but the opposite is also true for a broken one.

A bloated system is a broken system. Systems have to remain pliable and adaptable to the processes. If any meaningless formalities set in, or a meeting becomes more important than what is accomplished in a meeting, then the system is broke. A lean mindset is required where failures are addressed quickly.

REGARDING FAILURE

There are many witty sayings about embracing failure. Such as failing fast or failing forward, etc. Yes, we can expect failures at times. Especially if we are going to be innovative, we can expect to experience failures now and then. But the fact remains, failure is still exactly that- failure. It is not what we are striving for. We want success and the quicker we can rebound from a failed attempt the better.

When a failure occurs, it is important to not see it as a person but as an event.

Failure is an event, not a person. – *Zig Ziglar*

The failure might be a personal error, but we need to find the root cause. Did a person fail to follow the system, or did the system fail? The second thing to determine is if it was a predictable event or unpredictable.

These questions help cut to the core of a failure and give us the data we need to determine the best solution. When we can pull the team together to find a solution rather than pointing fingers, we can recover quickly and move on toward the success we all want.

FOUR DIMENSIONAL SERVANT LEADERSHIP

P *hil. 2:5-7 Let this mind be in you, which was also in Christ Jesus: ⁶ Who, being in the form of God, thought it not robbery to be equal with God:⁷ But made himself of no reputation, and took upon him the form of a servant, and was made in the likeness of men: (KJV)*

THE LEADERSHIP CRISIS

There is an overwhelming number of books on leadership. On December 29, 2017, Amazon listed almost a quarter of a million books under business management, and 27,000 of those books are on leadership.

It seems with all those resources we should have an abundance of capable leaders or at least a good grasp on what leadership is and how to develop it.

Yet, the lack of leadership was the third highest concern in the "Outlook On the Global Agenda 2015" report that was conducted by the World Economic Forum with 86% of those surveyed agreeing that we have a leadership crisis in the world today.

Do we really lack leaders? Or do we simply lack the kind of leaders that we would like to see?

I believe we have plenty of leaders. But there is a vast difference in the postmodern leader of today versus the leaders that came out of the first half of the 20th century. Today's leaders are simply the result of our beliefs and practice that has developed over the last fifty years, sometimes referred to as postmodernism.

At the core of postmodern thought is the questioning of truth. After the end of World War II, our thought process began to shift. Up until we dropped the atomic bomb, we had a primary belief that all advancements in technology and industry were for the betterment of mankind. Following the fears of the Cold War, our trust in authority diminished as we experienced Vietnam and the Watergate scandal and continued to do so as almost every type of leadership from politics to those in the church suffered from corruption and scandal. All this distrust helped fuel the sexual revolution of the sixties and social rebellion mixed with the even earlier feminist movement that resulted in a society that now questioned almost every moral truth that had been held unquestioningly for centuries.

As the theory of evolution gained ground in our public education, we developed even more questions and doubts about what we believed. Divorce and remarriage were no longer shameful in the community, and the church accepted the changes so as not to lose members. As adultery, homosexuality, and pornography increasingly plagued the church, the number of single-parent homes steadily increased.

During the nineties, the image of the male father figure continued to be diminished and was often depicted in movies and sitcoms as a bumbling and incompetent figure. In 2016, the U.S. Census Bureau reported that 17.2 million children were being raised in fatherless homes.

All these social elements along with the dramatic increase in personal technology devices obviously brought a whole world of new problems into the home and education system. From Ritalin to participation awards, we used whatever we could to try to help kids function better and feel good about themselves.

Now, I know that you're probably getting depressed just reading this, which is exactly the point. You cannot depart this far in belief and practice from the biblical model that God had established for the family and not expect any adverse effects in society. As society departs from biblical truths, so will the practices of servant leadership that you see modeled in scripture.

Instead, as we try to make our disadvantaged kids feel good about themselves at all cost and without taking responsibility for or having consequences for bad behavior, we will also be creating leaders that have the same mentality, attempting to be leaders only to benefit self. Our acts of service are too often evaluated by what the potential benefits or returns might be.

"True greatness, True leadership is found in giving yourself in service to others. Not in coaxing or inducing others to serve you."- *Oswald Sanders*

THE BOOK ON LEADERSHIP

I don't believe that we can find any book with better lessons on leadership than what we find in the Bible ranging from great examples of both leadership failures and successes in Moses, Nehemiah, and Solomon in the Old Testament to Paul's challenges in the New Testament.

Of course, Jesus, himself, is the ultimate example of what servant leadership really looks like. This type of leadership will influence instead of coerce. It will draw instead of push. It will serve and inspire others.

This type of leadership will produce people who are truly engaged and will endure the course because they believe in a vision that is bigger than themselves.

When your team becomes engaged with the vision of a company versus just being employed by a company, they become motivated by more than just a temporal reward, or weekly paycheck, as it might be. It becomes a cause involving something greater than a personal agenda.

One of my favorite models of servant leadership is what is shown in the Old Testament book of Ezekiel. Even though I believe this example relates more to church leadership, it applies well to the mindset of any Christian leader.

THE EZEKIEL LEADERSHIP MODEL

Ezk 1:10 As for the likeness of their faces, each had the face of a man; each of the four had the face of a lion on the right side, each of the four had the face of an ox on the left side, and each of the four had the face of an eagle. 11 Thus were their faces. Their wings stretched upward; two wings of each one touched one another, and two covered their bodies. 12 And each one went straight forward; they went wherever the spirit wanted to go, and they did not turn when they went. (NKJV)

Four similar creatures are also referenced in Isa. 6 and Rev. 4.

Each creature had four faces and were under the crystal firmament that was under the throne. In Revelation, each face is depicted as four individual creatures around the throne itself.

Various writers throughout church history and especially those of the early church have aligned these four faces with the four gospels. It is interesting, however, that many of them did not agree on exactly which face represented which gospel. Most depicted John as the eagle, and probably the most consistent today is the idea that Matthew depicts the Lion, the kingship of Christ, and Mark as the Ox and the servanthood of Christ. Luke is seen as depicting the man Christ and John as the eagle and divinity of Christ. As you study the Gospels, you begin to see the uniqueness of each one.

This description of the four creatures is what I believe to be a beautiful picture of both diversity and unity working in perfect harmony like any leadership team should.

First and foremost, I think these creatures in Ezekiel depict unity. They reached out their wings to touch one another. We could say they were voluntarily joined, yet each maintained its own direction as they moved in perfect unison as the spirit dictated. Their wings stretched upward toward the throne above, pointing to the one source of their strength and authority.

Ps. 28:2 Hear the voice of my supplications When I cry to You, When I lift up my hands toward Your holy sanctuary. (NKJV)

1Tim. 2:8 I desire therefore that the men pray everywhere, lifting up holy hands, without wrath and doubting; (NKJV)

Two of their wings covered their body. Being properly covered becomes consistent with modesty, submission and a willingness to serve without notice or attention to oneself.

As much as the creatures depict unity, I believe the faces depict diversity. Why is the gospel presented by four different men? Each one has a different emphasis or perspective and yet has a completely unified message.

If you have ever taken a DISC personality test, you can

quickly see how different each one of us is. Even more importantly, you can see how much we need diversity on our team to provide strengths where we are weak.

Every person will have his strengths, emphasis or angle that he sees as most important. It is only when we see the gifts of others as being as important as our own and are committed to operating in unison that we can really experience the strength and power of a leadership team.

If we begin to see our own angle or emphasis as being more important than any other, that ours is the leading cause, then we break the unity of leadership and become our own creature, a beast within the organization that does more damage than good. We invalidate our own role or ministry once we think it is more important than another's.

I believe, first and foremost, that this is God's design for His church, the body of Christ. Christ said He could only do what the Father told Him to do, and even so today, His body has to continue in complete subjection to the Father, each one submitting to one another in perfect unison so that the power of God can be manifested. There is no position in the church that is not subject to another in the church. If you are not truly subject to another part of the body, then are you truly a part of the body?

I believe this sets a scriptural precedence for our role in business leadership as well, always being under some authority and always seeking to make those over us successful.

Authority is one of the four key elements in our 4-dimensional leadership model.

FOUR DIMENSIONAL SERVANT LEADERSHIP

This four dimensional leadership model in Fig. 4.1 is represented as the central leadership plate in the Four

Dimensional Business Model in Fig. 2.1. It is the primary plate that holds together the central gear and keeps each business segment aligned and functioning together.

Fig. 4.1　© 2017 Leon Yoder

At the center of this leadership, plate is the mission statement for the business or organization that the leadership represents. See chapter two for more details on developing a mission statement. An effective mission statement will give clear direction to lead and guide them in making decisions that keep an organization headed in a consistent direction.

The four dimensions of this leadership model are the fundamental characteristics that will define the effectiveness of a servant leader. A leader that will continue to develop these four areas will continue to become a more effective leader.

AUTHORITY

AUTHORITY [uh-thawr-i-tee] the power to determine, or otherwise settle issues or disputes; jurisdiction; the right to control, command, or determine.

IN AUTHORITY OR UNDER AUTHORITY

Without authority, a leader becomes crippled and unable to do his job. The worst kind of delegation is when a person is given a job to do but not the authority to carry it through. Every team member should have a very clear understanding of what authority is given to them. What kind of decisions are they allowed and expected to execute?

Ronald Reagan said, "Surround yourself with the best people you can find, delegate authority, and don't interfere as long as the policy you've decided upon is being carried out."

We have all seen where authority was abused or misused and caused much damage. The key to authority in servant leadership is the manner in which this authority is used. It is the difference of seeing oneself as in authority or under authority.

One of the best examples of this is found in the Bible in Matthew 8:8 and the account of the Roman centurion who asked Jesus to heal his servant.

Mt 8 The centurion answered and said, "Lord, I am not worthy that You should come under my roof. But only speak a word, and my servant will be healed. 9 For I also am a man under authority, having soldiers under me. And I say to this one, 'Go,' and he goes; and to another, 'Come,' and he comes; and to my servant, 'Do this,' and he does it." 10 When Jesus heard it, He marveled, and said to those who followed, "Assuredly, I say to you, I have not found such great faith, not even in Israel! (NKJV)

Note that the centurion said he was also under authority, not in authority. Big difference.

He recognized that his power was not because of himself, but what empowered him was the authority of the Roman government above him. He recognized that Jesus' power also didn't come from himself but rather was given to Him by the authority above Him.

A leader who is not under authority is a dangerous leader indeed. We need to see leadership as a place of responsibility and not a place of power.

Being placed in a position of authority does not prevent us from making mistakes or needing correction at times.

Even the apostles made mistakes that required divine correction.

SEEKING HONOR

Luke 14:8 "When you are invited by anyone to a wedding feast, do not sit down in the best place, lest one more honorable than you be invited by him; (NKJV)

This verse sets a simple but profound standard for the servant leader. Our drive and motivation should be to accomplish our mission and not to accomplish prestige or position. We should be seeking to develop those around us with the intent that they will someday surpass us.

Are we okay with giving credit to where credit is due,

to recognize those who contributed to the success? This is crucial in building a team culture. A team where each one is not afraid to share their ideas knowing that the team leader will not try to take all the credit for themself.

We should always have a mindset that someone around us holds the solution to our next problem.

INFLUENCE

Influence [in-floo-uh ns] to move or impel (a person) to some action

The overall success of a leader could probably be measured most accurately by the degree of influence that the leader has. A leader cannot be a leader unless there are followers, and followers are obtained by influence.

Being a boss and being a leader are not the same thing. You can have people follow your orders simply because you have been placed in a position of authority over them.

I remember quite clearly one day when I asked my office manager to do a certain task for me. This was a task that was well within her usual realm of duties, but when I asked her if she could do this for me, she turned with a smile and asked, "why do you always ask us if we would do a task like this instead of just telling us to do it? What if we said, 'no, I don't really want to," she laughed. A couple of the other team members overheard this, and we all got a chuckle out of this. But I realized that day that my goal was to make each team member feel like they had ownership in the company and were so much more than just an employee. This was my mindset, and so, therefore, it reflected in how I spoke to them. I asked them in a manner like they really did have an option because I wanted them to do it because it was the best thing to do and not just because I was their boss and was requiring them to do it.

That day I realized how important it is to have the right mindset. Because no matter what words you say, you will portray your mindset to the rest of your team.

A servant leader will have a servant mindset and will lift up those who are around him and inspire and encourage others. For a leader to be able to do this, he has to be confident in his position and his ability.

Some might mistakenly think that having a servant mindset is being a weak leader. It is actually quite the opposite. It takes incredible confidence to be willing to lead by influence instead of leading by positional authority.

Being a servant leader does not mean that a person shirks their duty as a leader by making decisions based on popular opinion. A capable leader has to be strong enough to make the best choice whether or not it is the most popular. The best choice has to be based on wisdom and the understanding of the overall mission and values. What may appear to be successful today has to be evaluated through the lens of the long-term vision.

THE INFLUENCE OF WORDS

The tongue is powerful. Simple words can do great damage, but they can also be a great builder of influence.

The interesting thing is that the tongue is a terrible beast to tame, as it will spew forth the contents of the heart if placed under stress. We can try to trick the tongue and have it say what we want, but if it is not from the heart, it often loses its sincerity and says words that are either harsh or sound like flattery.

The work of influential words has to start in the heart to be truly successful. It can be difficult at times to change our heart about those around us, but being willing to engage people and taking an interest in those around us will change our attitude about them. Knowing what they struggle with and what they enjoy will help us to see others in a different perspective.

Utilizing the DISC model of human behavior can also be very helpful in understanding the differences in those around us and change the way we communicate with others. This might sound like it is ok to manipulate people, but there is a difference between motivating and manipulating.

To manipulate is to influence people in a way to gain an unfair advantage for us. DISC should be used to help us communicate our thoughts and ideas more effectively so that any person's motivation comes out of a better understanding of the goal rather than being coerced into doing something just to benefit us.

Manipulation will never result in long-term dedication.

Character is the driving force behind successfully influencing those around us.

INTEGRITY

INTEGRITY [in-teg-ri-tee] the quality of being honest and having strong moral principles; the state of being whole and undivided. The stability and cohesion of all the components that make up the whole.

Integrity is the soundness of our moral and ethical standards, our moral framework. Integrity is the bedrock of a leader's success. Integrity in the life of a leader is when the various parts of our lives are consistent with each other.

In recent years, I have seen where leaders were applauded for compartmentalizing the different areas of their life. This idea undermines the very concept of leadership integrity.

Would my children say that I am the same person at home that people see at church and the same person that you will see at my work?

It's important that these different areas of our life are aligned. Relationships in one will eventually affect the other areas.

Ever since the era of Watergate in the early 1970s, we have seen an ever-increasing number of scandals within leadership. These scandals have affected leaders in every area from the government to even the church. It has eroded confidence in authority for a whole generation.

I know the effect that this can have on us. The very pastor who baptized me, married my wife and me, and was a very influential mentor in my early spiritual life ended up in jail. He had an affair with another woman and was convicted on charges of financial fraud. He not only defrauded the church out of money but individuals within the church.

This type of scandal shakes the very base of our faith.

I have seen many other honorable men fall to scandals and especially sexual scandals.

We must recognize that the heart of man is desperately wicked, and without the cleansing power and work of Jesus Christ in our life, we will not be properly equipped to do battle against the enemy that wants to undermine our integrity.

The Bible tells us to resist the devil on every front except one. When it comes to sexual sin, we are told to flee.

So how can we, especially us men, prepare ourselves and protect our integrity? We know we are to flee sexual sin, but we also need to protect ourselves and put on the full armor of God.

I believe leaders have to establish certain priorities and principles if we are to remain pure and blameless.

THE GRAHAM/PENCE RULE

Vice president Mike Pence received much criticism from the press when they discovered that he had adopted the Billy Graham Rule regarding his interaction with other women in business. He would not have a one-on-one meeting with another woman without his wife being present. He would never attend an event where alcohol was served without being accompanied by his wife.

Was it because he was afraid he would be tempted to get drunk? Absolutely not. It was all about preserving integrity and avoiding all appearance of evil.

Other men have shared with me that they will never meet with a woman in an office where the door is closed and always have another person present when meeting one on one with the opposite sex.

The media has published all kinds of criticism about Pence claiming this rule restricts the advancement of women in the workplace. We have to be aware of the enemy who wants to destroy us. Let's not fool ourselves, it does not matter how conservative a church we attend, we are not immune from being tempted.

INITIATIVE

INITIATIVE [ih-nish-ee-uh-tiv] an introductory act or step; leading action. one's personal, responsible decision

Lack of leadership accomplishes nothing. There's probably no statement that is more obvious, but so many times, we know what should be done yet never take that first step.

When I was considering the different elements of leadership, there were so many that I thought would need to be included. Something like innovation is extremely valuable in leadership yet useless if there is no initiative behind it.

Leaders have to be innovative, but many innovative ideas never even make it to a drawing board because of the lack of initiative. All the creativity and ability in the world is worthless without initiative.

LET YOUR PAST DIRECT YOU, NOT DEFINE YOU

What keeps us from trying? Is it the fear of failure? The fear of failing is definitely a strong deterrent in attempting new things.

I believe that some of our biggest deterrents are the barriers that we create for ourselves.

We are more aware than anyone of our past failures. We see our faults and weak points, and we immediately have this list of baggage from our past that hinders us from taking a step into the future. We look at others and see only their successes and begin to believe that everyone else has it together except ourselves. This is one of the biggest lies that we tend to believe about ourselves and others.

Everyone else has as many faults and as much dirty laundry as the next person. If someone says they don't, let me just ask their spouse or a close friend. We are all imperfect and all have our weaknesses. Of course, some of those weaknesses might be more obvious than others! But unless we are willing to step out of our past and try, we will remain stuck where we are believing our own little lies.

We have to recognize that our past does not define us. The past is there to direct us and grow us. We have to be able to look at our failures objectively and analyze them. Why did that fail? What could I do differently next time to prevent this? Trials are training tools that help us build something bigger and better.

It takes initiative to try new things and to reach for that success.

It takes integrity to remain successful and remember that we do still have dirty laundry in the closet and that others we meet may have a lot more experience in an area about which we know very little. Keeping this in mind keeps us humble and inspires us to keep reaching out to the expertise of others.

RISK MANAGEMENT

Initiative without intuition is also quite deadly in its combination. We can have all the initiative in the world, but without having knowledge and understanding of the reality we are living in will result in being nothing more than a loose cannon. A loose cannon on deck is about as likely to sink your own ship as it is to sink anything else.

There are risks involved in just about anything we do. The key is properly evaluating and managing those risks. A few good questions can go a long way in tempering our ambitions and tethering them to reality.

What is the payoff or benefits that can be expected from this effort?

What does this specific success contribute to the success of our overall goal?

Is the value of the success in proportion to the risk attached to it?

How would this specific failure affect our overall goal?

Everything revolves around risk management. What

are ways you can minimize the risk? Even if it means sharing the success with others, could you recover if you took all the risk and failed? Does partnering in the project increase the potential success because of deeper resources?

Remember, 10 percent success is much better than 100 percent failure.

Understanding your own personality, strengths and weaknesses will give you valuable perspective on where to stretch yourself and where to hold back.

Either way, don't be afraid to step out of the crowd and take the initiative to try!

BYSTANDER EFFECT

Sometimes, the best way to grasp the meaning of something is to examine the opposite of it.

To do that, we will look at an intriguing phenomenon in the world of psychology known as the "bystander effect," which is quite opposite of taking the initiative.

One of the first incidents that inspired research on this was the 1964 murder of Kitty Genovese in New York City. Her brutal attack and murder were witnessed by numerous people, and yet, no one reported the incident. Investigators were appalled that no responded.

Numerous social experiments were conducted a few years after to try and understand what may have taken place.

Research has found that the larger the crowd, the less responsibility a person will feel to take the initiative to step out to help. Everyone tends to think that surely someone else is better qualified to help or has a better understanding of what is happening. We don't want to be the one who steps out and makes a fool of ourself.

It takes true initiative to be willing to speak up or step out, even if it is to simply ask a question and find out what the situation really is.

Even in the process of leading a group through a problem-solving exercise, a simple majority vote is not always the right solution. It is the leader's responsibility to take the initiative to implement what he believes will best accomplish the desired outcome.

SETTING GOALS

It takes initiative to set goals, and setting goals is at the very root of success. What is success if it is not arriving at some designated point? That designated point, or goal, can be anything we desire enough to put forth an effort to reach.

A desire without effort is wishing.

Or, as the French writer Antoine de Saint-Exupery wrote, "A goal without a plan is just a wish".

Our days are filled with goals, many of them small and reached without much planning or even thinking of them as goals, such as stepping out of bed or preparing lunch. If only all our goals were so easily reached!

It only takes a few failures for us to realize that any significant goal will require a significant plan.

Most goals can be obtained fairly easily if they are broken down into simple daily steps.

In 1981 George Doran introduced the S.M.A.R.T. acronym for establishing goals and objectives. The S.M.A.R.T. acronym has since taken on numerous variations of the original, which was Specific, Measurable, Assignable, Realistic, and Time-related. The numerous variations included a SMARTER acronym that included Evaluated and Reviewed by Graham Yemm.

Following is my own modification using the SMARTER acronym and adding a Reward to the mix.

SETTING SMARTER GOALS

- **Specific** The goal or destination needs to be specific. Without specifics, it remains a vague idea that becomes impossible to measure.

- **Measurable** Peter Drucker wrote, "you can't manage what you don't measure". Once you have specific steps that you can measure, then you likely have a goal that is attainable.

- **Attainable** The attainability of the goal, in spite of the best-laid plans, will not be attainable unless you have all the required resources.

- **Resources** The resources required to reach your goal can vary greatly. They might include having the right people, the right equipment, the right information, sufficient finances and sufficient training and stamina to reach the destination within the time frame.

- **Time-Frame** Without a time frame for the goal, it will be impossible to evaluate the proper resources. You may have the resources you need to start, but can you maintain for the extended time that may be required to reach the goal? A race that has no defined finish line cannot be properly prepared for, and progress or results cannot be properly evaluated if there are no checkpoints.

- **Evaluation** Both the progress and results should be evaluated. There are always variables in every equation, and properly evaluating the progress is crucial to completion. Just as runners evaluate their resources at certain laps or stages in the race, our resources need to be evaluated to ensure that all the steps can be accomplished with the allotted resources and time frame required to reach the final reward.

- **Reward** Every goal needs to have a definable reward. Whether it is a tangible reward or even emotional, it will be a factor in the final evaluation. What was the payoff? Was it worth the resources consumed? Was it worth the experience? Even things that may appear to be a failure, such as a race that was lost, may still have been worth the experience.

So, it is quite easy to see that there are great benefits to setting goals. The more difficult the destination, the greater the planning it takes to arrive successfully.

In fact, most business leaders would agree that goal setting is one of the most fundamental skills required in leadership.

It does help to also be aware that different personalities are motivated differently. Some will only need a year-end goal and have all the motivation they need. Others will need to break down the goals into weekly and even daily tasks to make it more effective. Either way, will require a plan.

So we have to ask the question, are goals ever unbiblical? How is the Christian to set goals?

Many are the plans in the mind of a man, but it is the purpose of the Lord that will stand. Proverbs 19:21 ESV

It is quite easy for us to select a few verses from scripture that support what we want to believe and run with it. Doing so, we could build two very opposing positions related to setting goals and making plans, etc.

What advantage would it be to us, though, if we were to convince ourselves of something that God did not intend? It is to our benefit to truly seek what God's desire is by using scripture to interpret scripture.

To better understand the opposing views, I created two personas to represent these.

FRANK

Frank is a devout Christian and has a high regard for scripture, believing it is God's word.

These verses have had a big impact on him.

Matthew 6:19 "Do not lay up for yourselves treasures on earth, where moth and rust destroy and where thieves break in and steal, 20 but lay up for yourselves treasures in heaven, where neither moth nor rust destroys and where thieves do not break in and steal. 21 For where your treasure is, there your heart will be also. ESV

Matthew 6:31 Therefore do not be anxious, saying, 'What shall we eat?' or 'What shall we drink?' or 'What shall we wear?' 32 For the Gentiles (the world) seek after all these things, and your heavenly Father knows that you need them all. 33 But seek first the kingdom of God and his righteousness, and all these things will be added to you. ESV

James 4:13 Come now, you who say, "Today or tomorrow we will go into such and such a town and spend a year there and trade and make a profit"— 14 yet you do not know what tomorrow will bring. What is your life? For you are a mist that appears for a little time and then vanishes. ESV

Romans 8:14 For all who are led by the Spirit of God are sons of God. ESV

Matthew 21:22 And whatever you ask in prayer, you will receive, if you have faith." ESV

BILL

Bill is a devout Christian and has a high regard for scripture, believing it is God's word.

These verses have had a big impact on him.

Proverbs 21:5 The plans of the diligent lead surely to abundance, but everyone who is hasty comes only to poverty ESV

Proverbs 6:6 Go to the ant, O sluggard; consider her ways, and be wise. 7 Without having any chief, officer, or ruler, 8 she prepares her bread in summer and gathers her food in harvest. ESV

2 Corinthians 9:6 The point is this: whoever sows sparingly will also reap sparingly, and whoever sows bountifully will also reap bountifully. ESV

Ephesians 4:28 Let the thief no longer steal, but rather let him labor, doing honest work with his own hands, so that he may have something to share with anyone in need. ESV

1 Timothy 5:8 But if anyone does not provide for his relatives, and especially for members of his household, he has denied the faith and is worse than an unbeliever. ESV

Matthew 21:22 And whatever you ask in prayer, you will receive, if you have faith." ESV

A BIBLICAL MIDDLE?

Just in reading each selection of verses, you can begin to imagine the different thought structures that will dominate Frank and Bill. Their daily decisions and overall approach to life will be completely different.

Is there not a ditch on either side of this street? Let's look at the potential error in either one.

Frank will rely on his feelings over his intellect. He believes that the Holy Spirit does not lead people to make plans but leads each one spontaneously. The danger here is the tendency to believe our feelings are infallible in sensing the leading of the Spirit.

Bill will trust his intellect over his heart. As the Word is written, so he believes and makes plans accordingly and is not easily deterred. The danger in this is to neglect the promptings of the Spirit in his daily walk.

If we commit our plans to the Lord and are willing to be flexible as He prompts us, we can walk in confidence and trust the plans that we have committed to the Lord and possibly stay out of either ditch.

Proverbs 16:3 "Commit to the Lord whatever you do, and he will establish your plans." ESV

Proverbs 3:6 "Trust in the Lord with all your heart and lean not on your own understanding; in all your ways submit to him, and he will make your paths straight." ESV

Psalm 127:1 "Unless the Lord builds the house, the builders labor in vain." ESV

Jeremiah 17:7 "But blessed is the one who trusts in the Lord, whose confidence is in him." ESV

1 Thessalonians 4:11 and to aspire to live quietly, and to mind your own affairs, and to work with your hands, as we instructed you, 12 so that you may walk properly before outsiders and be dependent on no one. ESV

CHAPTER 5

BUILDING A SUCCESSFUL TEAM

*E*phesians 6:7 *Work with enthusiasm, as though you were working for the Lord rather than for people. NLT*

THE END OF HIRING EMPLOYEES

The greatest challenges facing small businesses today are human resources. The era of hiring employees has come to an end. What worked in the past century will not work in this one. There is a very different mindset in today's worker than that of one hundred years ago.

The first half of the 1900's was the age of modernism. There was tremendous growth in the industrial world, and even though the workforce was growing rapidly here in America because of the high rate of immigration and the traditionally larger families, the unemployment rate in the first eight years of the last century was less than 3 percent. The work environment was completely different than what it is today. The work weeks were extremely long, and the conditions were generally not good. This was the age that inspired the creation of labor unions and, even later, agencies like the Occupational Safety and Health Administration (OSHA) and the Environmental Protection Agency (EPA) in the 1970's.

The corporations ruled. They had few rules and guidelines to follow.

By the late 1930's during the Great Depression, unemployment had reached 24.9%. Throughout the last century, we saw these numbers go up and down.

At the time of this writing in 2018, our economy is booming. Our unemployment rates have fallen from 10 percent to almost 4 percent in eight years coming really close to the numbers of a hundred years ago.

Because employment is based on supply and demand, a competitive market has prevailed. The higher the demand for labor, the higher the wage that is required to get skilled, qualified labor. This has remained the general rule throughout the modern age, and it continues to some extent. The cost of production labor has increased significantly in the past few years, especially in specific areas. I have seen expansion projects halted here in northern Indiana because of the lack of availability of suitable labor.

The increase in production labor cost has made it difficult for many small businesses to stay competitive in the labor market because product pricing is slower in catching up with labor costs. These problems seem to cycle and are probably not that abnormal overall.

There is, however, a new problem that has employers perplexed, which is the difficulty of hiring and keeping good employees in what would be considered the general labor job market, those employees outside of the highly specialized and high production jobs. The problem is usually just attributed to a bad work ethic of a generation with that generation being the millennials. A problem that could usually be fixed with a pay raise in the past doesn't seem to work anymore. It has attributed to one of the hottest topics today, employee engagement.

There is a very different mindset from previous generations, and like any complex issue, there is more than one contributing factor. I think it is fairly easy to recognize that a lot of people think differently than they did fifty years ago. Values that seemed to be absolutes are no longer common. Some of these same factors were covered in the beginning of the last chapter under Leadership Crisis.

This change is going to require successful companies to build teams rather than just hire employees. It requires a different mindset and leadership.

We look back at the industries of the early 1900's and are appalled at the work environment that employees endured, and we see the changes that companies made to improve those conditions. The corporate attitude was to just pay the employees a little more until they put up with the conditions. The improvements that were made caused the companies to look like they went from treating their employees a little better than slaves to actually caring about them to some extent.

The changes that companies will have to make today will look like a similar process to our great-grandchildren. I realize that we do not treat our employees like they did back then, but I believe the key will be that we have to actually put the golden rule to practice, to truly treat others like we would want to be treated. This might sound like we don't care about our employees, and I think many of our Christian business owners do care about them. But even then, probably many of us care more about whether they show up or not over what their life goals might be or the difficulties they might be experiencing in life.

The changes that are needed fit perfectly with the Christian ethics that we should already be applying anyway, so it should not be difficult to engage even further. It's something we've known for 2000 years. The world needs Christ and needs us to be more Christlike.

WHY WAGE ISN'T WINNING

The most difficult aspect of this whole employee engagement issue is that it seems that we are no longer able to simply pay off our employees, to simply entice them with more money. Sure, anybody will show up if you pay them enough, but what I'm referring to is a sustainable wage that is feasible for the company to pay and still stay in business. We all understand that as the cost of labor goes up so does the price of products and that, in turn, requires higher wages to afford those products, and the cycle continues. So it's never as simple as just raising wages.

So why has the dollar lost its advantage? Is it that this generation has higher morals and has put values above money?

I think it's pretty clear that we are not experiencing a revival in moral purity or an increased emphasis on family and other ideals that we usually attribute to values, quite the opposite if anything.

The fact remains, though, that there is some kind of value that is being held higher than just money.

So what is so different from life a hundred years ago? We will use some broad averages to make these comparisons, but in 1910, an average house would cost about 4.5 times your yearly wage, and today, an average house might be about 3.5 times your annual salary. So housing would be accordingly more affordable today than in 1910.

Gold has always been a fairly good standard through time and using that comparison, you could have purchased a little more than one half of an ounce of gold with your weekly salary in 1910, but today, you could buy approximately one whole ounce with an average week's pay.

One of the bigger changes in our wage dollar is the cost of our food. In 1910, it took about 43 percent of your weekly wage to feed your family, whereas today, it is closer to 25 percent to feed a family of about the same size. That percentage is probably even lower because, generally, we have smaller families than a hundred years ago.

These are rough figures, and there are many variables that would take a complete book to truly analyze, but it is quite clear that our basic survival is much more attainable with our wage now than what it used to be.

Simply put, in 1910 if you didn't work, you didn't eat. Though there may have been some food kitchens, you were not able to go file for an unemployment check, food stamps and various other forms of support that can be obtained more readily today.

Fundamental survival is no longer at the forefront of the average employee's mind. It is whether we can afford the latest iPhone or what size data plan we can afford.

Combine this with the mindset of a generation that has been taught that we need to put self first along with no absolutes in values but, instead, your own perception of what is good for you.

Oprah Winfrey summed up the sentiments of this generation when she made this statement at the 2018 Golden Globes, "What I know for sure, is that speaking your truth, is the most powerful tool that we all have." [emphasis added] This concept that truth is equal to our opinion gives credence to a generation that thinks they can choose what gender they are. This is the very core of postmodern thought and creates a vast gulf between that and the reality of the business world-a world that is constrained by real facts and figures. It is this generation that is entering the workforce and finding difficulty in adapting. Though they have an air of confidence, many of them are quite unsure of themselves, seeking something to give them a greater purpose, something that money is not able to purchase.

SEEKING SIGNIFICANCE

There are some fundamental desires that God has integrated deeply into our design. We were created in His image, and that image is a link to something of much greater importance. It puts a natural knowledge and desire of a greater purpose deep into each one of us. Every one of us desires to have a significant life, for our life to have more meaning than the glob of matter that evolution has suggested that we are.

Along with this significance, we also have a deep desire for joy. The fulfillment of these two desires is often interpreted by the world as fame and fortune. Fortune is seen as the means to happiness which does not replace joy by any stretch of the imagination even if it could be bought, which it, of course, can't. The list is staggering of the wealthy people who have taken their own life this past year because they were depressed and lonely and yet surrounded by fame and a lot of money. No, the fulfillment sought by people goes far beyond fame and fortune.

The primary answer to our employment crisis is embarrassingly simple. It's not a sophisticated 12-step growth program. Our employees simply have to feel the relevance of who they really are, to know and understand how their job impacts others. And for that to happen, they actually have to become relevant to us in ways that they never have before. They need a bigger reason than just a paycheck to come to work.

FINDING FULFILLMENT

We might think that fulfillment will look very different for each person, and it will to some extent. But fulfillment is simply the achievement of something desired. Though some people may have difficulty expressing any real deep desire, I believe that everyone desires to be significant in some manner. So we may need to train our people in ways we never had to before.

The first step is to teach why their job is important, to gain an understanding of how their work fits into the bigger picture, to know who else is affected by how they do their job, and how their job is an important part of what the company is trying to accomplish. They need to feel the responsibility of their significant portion of the work because that will allow them to participate in the success. This may seem like a given thing to us, but this is the bedrock that has to be well established if we are to help our team be successful.

Proverbs 13:12 Hope deferred makes the heart sick, but a dream fulfilled is a tree of life. (NLT)

It is easy to stop here, once we have established their vision and goals for the job. But we need to continue and help them establish a deeper mission and purpose in their life.

It might seem foreign to us as Christians to not have a more defined purpose in life. Not only do we have a purpose because of our understanding of God, but also if we are inspired enough to start a business, we already know what it is to have a desire or a goal to accomplish something. But for many young people, and even some older ones, there is a surprising lack of purpose. And if there's a lack of purpose in their life, there will be an even greater lack of purpose in their job. Ultimately our jobs are simply a vehicle to accomplish our life goals. If there are no real life goals other than to meet our basic living needs, then we will also have a greatly diminished drive to excel and advance in our career.

As Christians, it's easy to pass it off and say that, unless they become Christians as well, they simply won't have a greater purpose. There may be some truth in that, but I believe the scriptures are clear that we are called to help others along the way regardless of whether they are believers or not.

So how do we accomplish this?

As a business owner, the first instinct is to look for a ready-made program that we can have our managers implement and then move on to more important things. This is, however, the core of the problem. Unless we personally lead the way in taking a new interest in our team members, it will be another good idea for a program that failed.

We have to begin in building a culture, not from the ground up or even from the top down. But change has to start with us and grow outward. We have to acquire a team mindset with the idea that we are all working on this vehicle together, a vehicle that we believe will take us somewhere. We as a team may all have slightly different goals or destinations, but we are all traveling with the same vehicle.

DEFINING THE DESTINATION

Using the allegory of our business being a vehicle, we need to recognize that each one on our team has a destination, life goals that they want to reach. The better we understand each others' destination, the better we are able to modify our vehicle for the trip.

You might say that since I am the owner, I am the only one that really matters. Again, in some sense, it is true. You created this vehicle for your trip and your journey, and if it isn't working for the others, they can get off the bus! But the fact is, you can't get there alone.

So we had better figure out how to get this bus modified to take us all where we want to get to, or none of us are going to be successful. Now, there is the reality that if your company bus is headed to the tropics, and you have people on board who want to go to Mars, they are obviously on the wrong vehicle. It may actually hinder both of you from reaching either of your destinations. A simple fact is that your company will not be the perfect fit for everyone who comes along. It's important that we recognize that. Often times though, modifications can be made that are helpful to everyone's goals.

So how does this all look in a real-world company? Let's look at some examples.

The technology companies have definitely been the forerunners in trying out new policies and benefits to attract the younger workforce.

Netflix in California has no set work hours. Vacation days and work hours are not tracked, as the company only measures what people get done.

Starbucks offers a College Achievement Plan for all employees who work over 20 hours a week. This plan allows them to earn a Bachelor's degree through an online college with the tuition paid.

Are you ready for really crazy? A social media company here in our region provides their employees with unlimited paid time off.

I know, the first thought is that this could not possibly work! But a quick disclaimer is needed. If you try to implement this tomorrow morning and expect it to work, it probably won't. There are many ways that these types of benefits won't work. But the amazing thing is that there are companies that have done this successfully. That in itself merits a closer look.

One of our first thoughts is that people would abuse this. It is hard enough to keep productivity up when you require them to be there much less pay them even when they don't show up!

The problem is that we have become so used to depending on a punched time card to control our labor force, believing that if we require them to be at our workplace for enough hours, they will be productive. How many times have we seen employees start watching the clock at about 4 pm and try to look busy and being totally unmotivated to get anything done other than to punch their card at 5 pm? That results in a lot of wasted productivity.

What if the controlling factor was based on what was accomplished instead of a time card? The bottom line is that this is what every company wants-employee productivity.

I suggested to the owner of the social media company that they must have some pretty clear expectations set for their employees and that this model probably wouldn't work for a more traditional top-down management. His response was that it definitely doesn't work for everyone, but they have projects assigned to small teams, and then the work is divided up among themselves according to each one's talent and expertise.

So not only does this create a huge accountability factor, but it also capitalizes on the strengths of each team member allowing each one to do the work they most enjoy doing. This model utilizes some of the core ideals of Agile Project Management. Working with smaller teams is always more efficient and more accountable, capitalizing on the strengths of each person and where all tasks have some reference of time frame associated with them. Project cycles are kept short so that defects can be identified more quickly and again save wasted time.

Someone else had asked this same owner if he doesn't have people taking advantage of this policy. He said not at all. One of his team members was on vacation and kept emailing him, and he finally told her that he will disable her email if she sends him one more email! When people are engaged and love their work, they will be productive. Obviously, if someone didn't produce any work, it would become very obvious to the team because the close interaction also creates high accountability.

These new management models have only in recent years become more popular with mostly tech companies leading the way. But are these ideas brand new? Some of these ideas were introduced as early as the late 1800's by Mary Parker Follett who was born into a Quaker family in Massachusetts. She was a social worker in Boston and through her writings became known as the mother of modern management.

She contributed greatly to what is today known as the win-win philosophy in conflict resolution and was a pioneer in what developed into matrix-style management utilized by General Motors and Dupont in the 1920's. Follett promoted a more cooperative approach to problem-solving that allowed the individuals to participate and take ownership in the solution rather than just follow orders. She argued that the employee should not be treated as "under" the employer but both become subject to the situation at hand and let the situation dictate the solution. Today, teams that utilize Agile methods such as Scrum depend on the expertise of the team members to critically analyze and evaluate the issues they encounter during each sprint or short phase of the project. It puts more responsibility on the team members, but in return, they feel a greater ownership.

OWNERSHIP & OPEN BOOK MANAGEMENT

Another model that is becoming increasingly popular and referred to by some as Open Book Management was first used by Jack Stack when he took over Springfield Remanufacturing, an ailing division of International Harvester. He created a new style of management that was very successful for him based on building a culture of ownership by educating each employee how to read their profit and loss statements and having them know how their job contributes to the bottom line. Their pay was also based on the companies profitability, and everyone shared in these profits. The name is a bit misleading as it involves so much more than just exposing your books to your employees. The term that Stack used to describe this approach was The Great Game of Business and probably gives a better indication of the philosophy behind it than simply Open Book management. My warning would be to not try to implement any of this unless you fully understand his whole model because just opening your books and thinking things will change is not reality. You might experience change, but probably not for the better. The success he has had, though, reinforces one of the core concepts here on building a culture of ownership. Ownership is not developed overnight, and it will look different depending on the type of business you have.

The incentive plan that I used in our sign shop was

in some ways similar to some of the previous ideas. I established an incentive plan that was based on the gross sales. So, we would let everyone know exactly how much we billed each week. We used a spreadsheet to calculate their bonus. We entered each person's hours, and it would establish our breakeven point based on our overhead and labor costs. Using the wage to sales ratio that was standard for our industry, we would start paying bonus after our sales passed the breakeven point. Once the sales crossed the second level, an even higher percentage was added to their wage. This suddenly made every employee invested and concerned about how much we were going to be able to bill for the week. They made the decisions whether they were going to try and finish a job for the week or not. I no longer had to be checking every week to make sure they were producing enough to keep us in business. If they didn't produce enough for us to stay in business, they were not going to be making very much money either.

There are many companies that are putting ideas like this into practice, some with greater success than others. I have heard of the failed attempts as well. There are always many factors at work that make these things successful. The important thing is to know that they are possible.

Changing the work culture of a company will not be accomplished in one week, that's for sure. But it does require that a first step is taken to start.

SIMPLE STARTS

There are some easy and simple ways to get started in building that culture. Food is one of those things.

One local company provides a complete meal every Friday for their employees. Food brings people together, and it shows a level of care from the owners that cannot be compared to money. It also worked well for this specific company because they had a small commercial kitchen on the premises.

A very successful entrepreneur told me years ago that one of the most effective ways to build employee gratitude is to have the owner himself fire up a grill on a Friday and grill burgers for his employees. That creates more value than any reasonable raise could ever do.

For other companies, it might be a company fishing trip or summer picnics where their whole families can be involved. It's important that events like these are valued by the employee, or it might be seen as a costly extravagance. This is probably more relevant to the smaller companies.

Some companies will pay their employees for hours they spend on community projects.

At one time, I had a few employees who were interested in doing some short-term mission work, and we started a policy that gave them paid time off in addition to their regular vacation pay. This was consistent with our vision as a company and was good for everyone.

In summarizing these concepts there are a few core principles that we can establish.

The first is significance.

Each of these models gives the team members a feeling of significance, understanding very clearly what they are contributing to the company. They know how their work relates to each of their team members and the overall company. They know that the decisions they make will really matter and will contribute to either the success or the failure of the company.

Second, the success has to be measurable. Every individual needs to know whether they are succeeding or not.

This is usually done with profit sharing incentives, etc., but might be done in some other ways as well.

Have you ever been part of a group that decided to play basketball, softball or maybe even volleyball, and someone got the great idea that we are going to just play for fun and not keep score. There is absolutely no quicker way to kill a game than to not keep score. In a matter of minutes, you will see people looking around to see what else might be taking place that is of greater interest, a little like people beginning to watch the clock about an hour before quitting time, wondering what might be the most creative way to kill the next hour until it's time to punch out. Mentally, they already left and will not only be unproductive but will probably strike up a conversation with someone else and keep them from being productive as well.

Thirdly, they need to be connected to the cause of the company and really understand the core values, the mission, vision and purpose statements of the company. Simon Sinek covers this topic well in his books on establishing your "why."

You have to know why you do what you do. Not being a natural morning person, I like to refer to this as, "what gets you out of bed in the morning?" What makes it worth all the challenges you face in small business? Once you know, you have to sell this vision to your team.

The last method, but definitely not the least, is to interview your team members and find out what their specific goals or dreams are and then help them set a plan in place to make it happen. Maybe it means providing some resources to the company to help find some online classes and making it possible for them to advance their education. The education can make them more valuable to the company, or if it's in a completely different field, it might mean that they will leave your company once they have accomplished that degree. That should not hinder us from helping because they will be better team members during the time that they are working for you. An associate of mine helped his employee reach her dream of buying a horse. He helped her plan for it, and they accomplished it.

These concepts are presented as ideas for starting points with enough information to help you ask the right questions. Changes, or at least major changes, come hard. I imagine it a little like conducting an orchestra. It takes a lot of finesse, time and coordination to make it happen. It starts with the little wins.

PERSONALITIES AND PLACEMENT

Understanding the different personalities of people and how those fit into a job position is some of the most useful knowledge your human resources department can have. Being a certified consultant for the DISC Model of Human Behavior, I am, of course, a little biased and believe DISC to be the most useful of the personality models for both business and everyday life. The DISC model starts with a very simple basis that is easy to remember and is easy to apply in everyday interactions without having everyone you meet to fill out an assessment form. But it still has the much more detailed assessments available for deeper studies.

Before I continue, let me clarify my use of two words that people will sometimes use differently than what I do here-personality and character. I view personality as the traits and natural tendencies that are hardwired into our being. Even though we can learn to utilize more of our less dominant traits, it usually feels more stressful. Character, on the other hand, is developed and can be more easily modified with practice and training. Though character can be modified, the changes usually don't come easy and won't happen at all unless the person really desires change.

I always thought that employment was all about the right skill sets until I had to hire employees and started training people, then I realized the value of character. A good character can usually be trained for just about any skill, but a bad character often remains a bad character.

The DISC model is primarily four parts that are the combination of either Outgoing or Reserved and People-oriented or Task-oriented as shown in the diagram below.

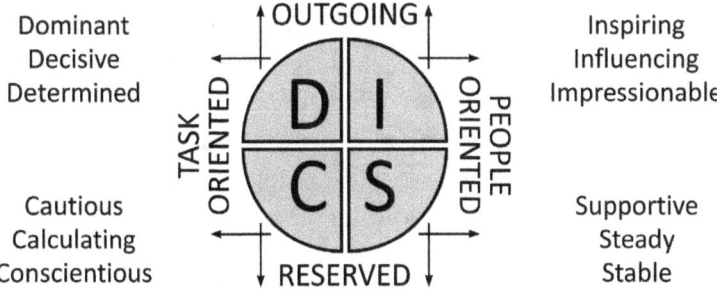

Each of our personalities are made up of a combination or blend of these four traits.

A strong D personality is both an outgoing and task-oriented person, where an I personality is also outgoing but is more people oriented.

Both the C and the S personalities are more reserved with the S being people-oriented and the C more task-oriented.

Understanding the strengths of the different personality types helps us place these people in the right positions. A high I personality will probably excel in a sales position and feel very fulfilled interacting with people all day, where a C type would probably want to do the paperwork and make sure it's all filed correctly. If you want someone to lead a project and make sure it gets done, a D personality will usually work great where an S might feel more comfortable in a supportive role.

If you switched any two of these positions you will end up with people in a highly stressed situation. It's not that they wouldn't be able to do the job, but it would not be a good fit long term because of the stress and dissatisfactions that it would cause.

The Carnegie Foundation has determined according to their studies that 85% of the success in the workplace is dependant on relational skills and only 15% relates to the technical skills. Considering that companies generally focus on increasing the technical skills of their employees but hardly ever have programs in place to increase the soft skills of both their managers and employees, it is clear that training in soft skills, such as communication, leadership and understanding people, can have a dramatic impact on our success.

CHAPTER 6

PRODUCT, PRICE & PROMOTION

*L uke 19:15 When he returned, having received the king-
dom, he ordered these servants to whom he had given the
money to be called to him, that he might know what they
had gained by doing business. (ESV)*

PASSION OR PRACTICAL

You have this great idea for a product or new service! It
keeps burning in your mind, and you start making notes
and sketches relating to it. It wakes you up at 2 a.m., and
you know you have to go write down some more notes on
it.

Many people might not be able to relate to this type of
thing, but entrepreneurs are very familiar with it. It's how
many of their businesses are formed-with those 2 a.m.
revelations.

Some that already have a great paying job might say,
"yeah, that was a great idea" but then not do anything with
it until it goes away. But for many of us with this afflic-
tion, it doesn't go away as easy as that.

Here is the difficult thing, and we have to be to analyze
it objectively. Is it really a good idea, and even more
importantly, is it a good idea for me? Does it fit into the
company I already have, or would it require a new ven-

ture or organization to develop it? What percentage of this idea is driven by passion and how much by practicality?

Granted, you should have some of both, but passion has a strange ability to often overrule the practical side of us. The ideas of passion are the ones that often turn into hobbies, sometimes unintentional hobbies. There is a time and place for those projects, projects that we feel have a greater cause than profit, and we recognize that if we do them we don't do it for money. Even if it is a noble cause or has spiritual benefits, is it in line with what God has called me to be right now? Does it fit my calling to my family, church and business? I have found that God's answers often come to me through my spouse or some trusted brother in the faith. I think this might be so that we have to rely on each other, and it's a way that God keeps us accountable to one another. It really becomes a beautiful way that our faith integrates with our whole life.

So what if it passes the practical test, and it's a product that we believe we need to analyze further?

OUR ATM RESOURCES

There are three basic resources that we need to look at in considering to add a new product or service to our business. The first resource needed is **Area**. Do we have the sufficient area or space required to add this product? Can we reorganize and maybe even cut a less desirable product that never had the potential of as much profit as this one? Do we have room to expand? How much space or area will it require in the first year and in five years if it would grow? Could the growth be handled if needed?

The second resource is **Time**. We are all limited to 24 hours each day, no matter how well we use it or however we may manage to squander it. For most of us, it seems that we have already allotted all the time we have to current obligations. Does what we want to do rank important enough to either delegate something else that we are currently doing, or are we willing to recognize that something else will be left undone? Being a CS personality, saying no is not one of my strong points, as it is for most S type personalities. But one thing I try to remind myself of is that for every yes that I say I am also saying no to something or someone else by default. To often, that someone else will be those whom we love the most! Realizing this has made it easier to say no at times.

The third resource is **Money**. It is not unusual to estimate too low the amount of money or capital that will be required to fully launch a new product, especially if the product is going into a new market and does not fit into your existing sales network. You will have the obvious things such as research and development, time and materials, then there might be new branding or packaging to develop. You may have new sales training and maybe staff to sell it not to mention the costs of setting up new production if it's required. An ideal service or product will be able to utilize some, if not most, of the existing infrastructure that you already have.

The area that is usually not included in the initial capital funding plans are growth funds. Once a product is sent to market and it really takes off, it can cause some major cash flow problems because of the sudden additional materials that need to be purchased and converted into product. The time it takes for all that cash flow to cycle through can take its toll on a small business.

So always carefully check your ATM for sufficient resources of Area, Time and Money.

PRICING FOR PROFIT

Before you start selling your product or service, you have to know how much you are going to sell it for, correct? So how do you establish this price? Is it based on being a dollar less than what your competition is selling the same product for?

Are there features that set your product apart from what is already on the market? If you are simply selling more of what is already available, you will need to make sure that the market is expanding sufficiently, or you have managed to find a more efficient way to produce it or have some advantage other than simply being a dollar less than the next person.

Your product needs to be priced based on the profit you need to generate. Granted, you do have to consider the competition and analyze the price point for your product in relation to the market. Unless you sell your product with a profit margin that is sufficient enough for operating and growing your company, you will be destined to fail from the beginning.

Usually, it is pretty easy to determine the cost of producing a product. You have the cost of the raw materials and the labor to convert it. The more difficult part is to determine the cost of your overhead and how that translates into the cost of the product. In addition to the production costs, there are usually marketing costs that are not figured into the price as well as other overhead, and sometimes, maintenance and replacement costs for equipment have to be included if the production is equipment intensive.

DETERMINING OVERHEAD

To determine your overhead costs, you have to consider the cost of everything that is not directly related to producing that product or service. Basically, this includes labor that you cannot bill for any costs that you cannot directly pass on to the customer.

These costs include the utilities and rent for your facility. Even if you already own the building and have no debt on it, you still need to figure the cost of that building spread out over a period of time. The operations in that building have to produce enough profit to pay for such a building.

Other costs include any administrative people such as secretarial work, bookkeeping, accounting, engineering or product development, marketing and other management wages and owner salaries that may not be directly related to producing your product.

Office supplies, production equipment, company vehicles, taxes and such all contribute to the costs of overhead.

Most of these costs would be considered fixed overhead cost. The cost of sales and advertising has to be included as well, But, sometimes, this is established as a percentage of the product cost to allow for those costs to fluctuate along with the volume of sales.

Once you know all these costs, you can divide this monthly cost into the number of days you are open for business and get a daily cost of operation. This method might work well for retail and some service-oriented businesses. Even for retail environments, it is helpful to know what your operating cost per square foot is for each day and each week.

PEER POINT

Alvin Miller – Davis Mercantile, Shipshewana, IN

———

Peter Drucker would say that you can't manage what you

don't measure. So, we measure every square foot of each department in our retail space. Then taking our fixed overhead costs, we know what each square foot of space is costing us per day. We then track our sales per department and know how much profit per square foot is generated in each department. Sometimes rearranging those departments can make a difference in sales. Sometimes the areas you think are doing pretty good are actually not producing the profit per square foot that you should be producing. Those numbers keep it real.

UNIT COST

There are a number of ways to determine the unit cost of your product.

A simple method is to take your total overhead cost, your direct labor costs and your materials cost for a specific period of time and divide by the number of units produced.

Another method is to find your total overhead cost by adding your fixed overhead costs with your labor costs and any other costs accrued for a specific time period such as one week. You can then divide your total overhead dollars by the material dollars for that period and determine the overhead cost per material dollar.

Example:

If total overhead cost is $10,000 and the dollar amount of production material used for all products is $50,000, calculate the overhead cost per material dollar as $10,000/$50,000 = $0.20 per material dollar.

Regardless of how you break it down, you have to be sure to allow for overhead costs and remember to add in your profit margin to determine your selling price.

Another point to remember is that there is a difference

between the retail and wholesale price of a product. if you are selling wholesale, you may want to establish an MSRP or Manufacturer's Suggested Retail Price that reflects the appropriate retail profit margins for your product.

If you manufacture a product that you both wholesale and sell retail, which is generally not a good practice, it is extremely important that you sell your retail product at the MSRP price to protect your wholesale customers. To determine an appropriate margin to use to establish the MSRP can be difficult and varies on the market, but many retailers require anywhere from 40-100 percent margin.

MARKET PRICE

Unless you are in a market where you have hardly any competition, it can be challenging to determine the right market price for your product. You should always seek to be competitively priced, but I do see many small businesses sell themselves short because they think they have to be the lowest priced product on the market to be able to sell it. Find those other values that you offer either in or with your product, whether that might be higher quality materials, better service, better design or whatever it might be other than just price because there will always be someone who will try to make your product for a dollar less than you do.

PEER POINT

Alvin Miller – Shipshewana, IN

My father had a pallet manufacturing company, and I remember one day a client called and asked for a specific kind of pallet. My father gave him a verbal quote while he was still on the phone, and the client said that one of our competitors sells the same pallet for less money. My father quickly responded by asking why are you calling us? The client replied and said that the competitor is currently out of stock. Oh, I see, my father said, Yes, our pallets also cost much less when we don't have them!

PRODUCT MARKETING

The terms sales and marketing are often confused. Marketing pertains to all the efforts put forth to expose your company and product to potential clients. Most of these efforts are usually in some form of advertising. Marketing can be much more than simply placing advertisements, though it takes on many forms, some of which may include branding, digital, social media, email, direct mail, broadcast, word-of-mouth, point of purchase, content, trade show, signage, newsletter, event, and the list goes on and on.

If we think of marketing as fishing, marketing is everything we do to catch the interest of the fish from finding the right lake to the lure we choose and everything up to the point that the fish nibbles your bait and establishes a lead. Everything else from setting the hook to getting the fish into the boat is called sales.

Anyone who shows an interest in your product becomes a lead with sales being the interaction you have with that potential lead to try and close the sale.

Marketing can feel a little overwhelming at times because the radio salesperson says that radio is the best way to advertise, the newspaper says that print still works, and the web designer says you have to be online or you won't survive these days. It's difficult to sort through it all and not get lost in the maze or, even worse, go broke advertising!

Every marketing person has their favorites, and I have learned that regardless of what anyone says, almost anything can work if it's done right or done brilliantly. In the same instance, the best platform can be disastrous if it is done badly. So, we will try to break done the marketing process into four segments that I've called Four Dimensional Marketing.

DEFINING YOUR NICHE

The first question I usually ask a client is, "why should I buy this from you?" What sets you apart from your competitor? What need, want or emotion does your product or service fulfill that your competitors do not?

There is an emotional buy-in on almost anything we purchase. We buy organic food to keep our family healthy. We buy the nicer life jacket because we not only want to keep our children safe but we don't want them to be made fun of. We buy the fast food because it's more convenient, and we don't want to put up with our kids fussing. This is where we choose one priority over the other, as the fast food is not as healthy, but it saves me the hassle. I want to save money, but I will buy convenience. There are many tradeoffs that we make with many of our purchases. Knowing what those tradeoffs might be for the product or service you offer can help you develop your marketing message.

You always focus on the benefits of the products. What will it accomplish for the buyer? What problem are you solving for that person?

Generally, if a lower price is your only advantage, then you are not establishing a long-term market niche, because there will always be someone else who will try to sell it for a dollar less. They may not succeed for very long, either, but may succeed long enough to put you out of business.

Knowing your competition is important, but there is a danger in getting too caught up with the competition. I know of small business owners who felt that they had to put the competition out of business and lost focus on just being a leader in the market. If a company will focus on being the best they can be, providing the best product and service at a competitive but sustainable price, the competition will take care of itself. Be a leader in your market instead of chasing the competition. As soon as your focus changes to your competition, you have begun chasing instead of leading. Market leaders are original. They set the bar for the market.

DEMOGRAPHICS

Knowing the demographics of your potential buyer is the next step. The better you have defined your niche, the better you will determine the demographics of your perfect client.

Create a persona or even multiple ones to fit the profiles you come up with. Create a name and an age and whatever other information that you believe would define your perfect client. Select the area that your client will live in, what their family might be like and what age their children might be. Where does this client go throughout the week? What income level are they, and where do they like to shop and go out to eat? What do they listen to on the radio, or do they read a certain magazine because of their interests?

Once you can determine these various lifestyle traits, you can start to look at their pain points and see how your service or product could solve some of their problems.

I read an account of a painter who was targeting retired

people who needed repainting in their homes but would not want to do it themselves. He discovered that many in his demographics were struggling to adapt to the new smartphones and figuring out how to do email, etc., so he offered a free class at the library to teach people how to set up their email and how to navigate their smartphones. After a while these people would ask, "hey, why are you doing this and not charging anything for it?" It gave him an opportunity to share what he does for a living and he handed out cards and told them if they knew any friends who needed painting that he would love a referral. They were more than happy to refer someone that they now knew and trusted.

As you discover the specific problems you are helping to solve for your clients, you may even go back and tweak your product to make it even more appealing to your new clientele.

DESIGNING YOUR CAMPAIGN

Once you really understand the problems you are solving and who you are solving them for, you can start to put together an advertising campaign. This might be printed ads, signs, brochures, radio ads, direct mail or digital internet advertising. Whatever it might be, it will need to be portraying the right message and designed to grab the attention of your potential clients. This only becomes more difficult as time goes on because everyone is being bombarded with so many advertising messages these days that we have effectively tuned most of it out.

It is important to design your advertising with a call to action in it – some reason for the viewer to act now rather than later. Even then, it is highly unusual for anyone to respond to the first viewing of the offer. We are so used to seeing ads multiple times that we seldom feel a need to act immediately unless it is something we really want to purchase. The only exception might be a point of sale advertising that is geared toward an impulse buy, but even many of those items are being promoted in other places first and exposing us to them in some other media or printed flyers before we come into the store. The more impressions that we can create for our product the greater the chance of converting to a sale.

DEPLOYMENT AND TRACKING

Deploying the plan and tracking the results are next. Every marketing program has its limits, and that limit is usually defined by the budget. Trying to advertise everywhere to everyone and hoping something works is a shotgun approach and is usually done when there is no plan. If something does happen to work, it becomes almost impossible to track and figure out what was or wasn't successful.

Placement and tracking are crucial. The more detailed the plan, the easier it becomes to track the return on investment (ROI). Tracking can be difficult at times but is well worth the time it takes to gather the data. Sometimes, you simply have to ask every client how they found you. If you can track your advertising, then you can repeat and expand on what was successful and grow your sales much quicker than taking a shotgun approach and never being quite sure what works and what doesn't.

Online tracking is much easier to do because you have a digital trail that can be tracked with tracking pixels and Google Analytics. Most email newsletter software has tracking features built right into it and enables you to see who opens the emails etc. Web analytics can also be used to some extent for printed advertising if you keep track of what areas you are doing a direct mail piece you can see if traffic picked up in those specific geographical areas during the time of the mailing.

It seems like marketing the product should surely be the hardest part of the complete marketing and sales cycle, but sometimes dealing with the customers can prove to be quite challenging in itself.

Most business owners know that we sometimes have to go the second and even third mile to try and please our clients, but sometimes... sometimes the customer is wrong.

THE CUSTOMER ISN'T ALWAYS RIGHT

The term "The Customer Is Always Right" was coined around 100 years ago by either Marshall Fields or his employee, Harry Gordon Selfridge, and first used by Marshall Fields & Company in Chicago. Selfridge was also the first to use "Only _X_ Shopping Days Until Christmas" to promote Christmas sales which caught on elsewhere about as quickly as the first term.

"The Customer Is Always Right" represented a much-needed shift in customer service in the late 1800's. As I understand, this was an era when the buyer had few rights. So, this new phrase ushered in a new benchmark for customer service for the next century.

It worked as a great axiom in training employees on how to handle customers. However, it became so widely used in our society that today our customers now believe it to be a universal truth, which is far from what it was intended to be. It has now become a license for customers to be rude and make all kinds of unreasonable demands.

There are a few things we need to understand in dealing with clients.

RESPECT

Our employees deserve to be treated respectfully.

Yes, even by our customers. Our employees are no less valuable than our customers and even more so because it will generally cost the company more to replace an employee than to replace a customer. However, regardless of the financial value, each employee, as well as our customers both, have a right to be treated respectfully.

So when management takes the side of a customer who chooses to treat an employee rudely and without respect, they will in the same sense demean the employee. It is hard, if not impossible, to build employee morale when managers don't stand behind their employees.

Now granted, if the employee has not handled the situation properly according to company policy and was rude to the customer, that is reason enough to terminate their employment and seek amends with the customer. But there are those rare occasions when we simply have to let the customer go.

Unreasonable Expectations

Yes, our customers are not always rational in their expectations.

Thanks to our marketing and sales people, not to mention politicians, lawyers, and news reporters, we tend to skew people's expectations with our over-ambitious sales pitch. Sadly, we tend to manipulate our graphs and charts to prove whatever point we want to make. Our product labels and sales materials are designed to entice people into buying our product over the competition. We naturally tend to oversell and, of course, not draw attention to the drawbacks of our products and services.

It is our reasonable duty to try to make every customer satisfied. No business owner likes to see a customer unsatisfied. But the brutal truth remains that a company does have a limited amount of resources and there will be that certain occasion where you simply have to let the client go and know they are just not the right customer for you.

There was this customer that had bought Brand X horse feed from the local feed store and came back later and said that their horses got sick from it and wanted to be reimbursed and costs covered.

The sales rep from Brand X became involved with the situation and tested the feed and made sure that the feed was to the exact specifications of all their feed and determined that their feed had nothing to do with it.

The feed store owner, not wanting to have a displeased customer, suggested that even though they did no wrong that maybe he should still refund the money.

The sales rep responded saying, "The dollar amount is not the issue at all. The amount would be insignificant to Brand X. However, if we refund the money, it will still not change the customer's opinion of Brand X."

If anything, it will simply reinforce in the customer's mind that Brand X was wrong, even though they weren't.

The owner of the feed store agreed that the sales rep was correct, but later he still refunded the client's money out of his own pocket and chose to suffer the loss, knowing he went above and beyond what was required.

Reflecting on this and some other instances like this, it is pretty easy to make a decision what you believe is right for the business, but the Christian faith isn't always based on what we think makes sense but rather what the Spirit prompts us to do.

I Corinthians 6:7 Now therefore *there is utterly a fault among* you, *because ye go to law one with another. Why do ye not rather take wrong? why do ye not rather suffer yourselves to be defrauded? (KJV)*

In processing this, it seems I always end up with another question. At our sign shop, we always took the position that we would not take anyone to small claims court to try and collect a debt, and there were certain debts that we ended up writing off. Having a policy like this kept us a little more aware of what projects we started without down payments and also how comfortable we were in letting customers create charges.

NOT KNOWING WHAT IS NEEDED

There are times that our potential clients simply don't have enough knowledge of the product to make the right decision. They may have misconceived ideas about what will be effective.

Part of the mission statement of our sign shop was "Our success depends on how well we accomplish our client's goal". I found that it was important to find out what the customer wanted to accomplish with the signs or graphics they were ordering. It was not uncommon to find out what they were trying to order was not going to work. So, this would give us an opportunity to educate them on why it should be done a certain way, and most of the time, we prevented a dissatisfied customer. There were times when the customer insisted on how they wanted it, and that still allowed us to protect ourselves from them coming back to us for something that didn't work.

This, of course, doesn't mean that we never made any mistakes, either, but we always attempted to help them accomplish their end goal.

CHAPTER 7

DEFINING SUCCESS

 *atthew 25:21 His lord said to him, 'Well done, good and faithful servant; you were faithful over a few things, I will make you ruler over many things. Enter into the joy of your lord.' NKJV*

ENTITLEMENT

Growing up in our Amish Mennonite culture, I now realize the advantages I had with what I thought were disadvantages at the time.

I may well have been the only Amish boy that dreamed of attending MIT and becoming a robotics engineer. I could have dwelled on the disappointment of not being able to go through high school and on through college. I could have used this as a crutch and excuse for any failure I encountered for the rest of my life. I didn't have a fair chance, etc, etc.

That in itself was a great gift. I understood from childhood that life was not exactly fair, but I also understood that it was not a handicap either.

I remember I was around 20 years old and had been working at a tool and die shop for a year or two and had to make a decision about enrolling into their apprenticeship when I realized I didn't want to be a machinist the rest of my life.

I had been offered a job at a van conversion company building custom van campers, one at a time. I would basically build one conversion from start to finish, having to do everything from electrical and plumbing to building the cabinets and final finish. I felt like I may be jumping into the deep end of the pool without knowing if I could swim.

On my last day at the tool and die shop, I was talking to one of the journeymen about my concerns on whether I could handle this new job I was taking.

Without looking up he stated, "you will do just fine".

I was taken aback, but his matter of fact tone of voice sounded like he really knew something I didn't.

I said, "What do you mean?"

He turned and looked at me and said. "I have a boy your age. When I ask him to take out the trash, he still asks me 'why do I have to do that'? You have already figured that out."

I think I thanked him. I'm not quite sure as I walked away befuddled. I think it took me ten years to figure out what he meant.

I had just assumed that nobody owed me anything and that I was going to have to work for whatever I got. I even assumed that I was at a slight disadvantage and would probably have to work harder than the next person because I didn't finish high school like most of my peers. Thanks to my hardworking father, I had not yet discovered this dastardly little attitude called "Entitlement".

Your biggest advantage is to assume you have a disadvantage.

Sensing a slight disadvantage, for one, keeps us humble. It makes us try just a little harder and keeps us looking up to those around us, ever seeking to learn from our peers. It's the overconfident hare that loses the race to the turtle.

DEFINING SUCCESS

We all desire to be successful. But how do we define what true success is?

Is there a universal benchmark for success?

According to a dictionary, the simple definition of success is, "the accomplishment of an aim or purpose".

So in order to define success, we will need to have a clear understanding of our aim or purpose.

Now, I realize the aim and purpose of people will probably be as varied as the number of people that you would ask. But I believe we can at least bring some direction to what our aim and purpose should be, especially from a Christian viewpoint.

I would like for us to consider that our aim and purpose may have been affected by one of the biggest lies that is perpetuated here in the U.S. and is at the very core of the "American Dream". I believe we Christians have even influenced some of our children with this lie that "you can be anything you want to be".

We do have the freedom in this country to pursue whatever dreams we wish to pursue. But the fact remains that we are limited to what we can be. Not all of us can be President of the United States. Most of us will never be an NFL linebacker or NBA superstar.

The real appeal of this lie is that we can be the masters of our own destiny, unaccountable to God, doing only what we deem best.

This does not mean that we cannot pursue great things or even achieve great things. No, the truth is, if we are diligent in developing the talent and abilities that God did give us, every single person can achieve great success. It doesn't matter where you were born or in what condition. Each one of us has been created to do things that no one else but us can do! We each have a purpose that no one else can fulfill.

Success is not limited to and may actually have quite little to do with what most of the world would see as success.

Success in the world's eyes is generally related to how much fame and wealth a person has accumulated. But in reality, I have seen famous, wealthy people who were complete failures.

How can I say this?

It is quite simple. Success is the accomplishment of an aim or purpose. I am sure that every one that has sought fame and wealth envisioned that they would be happy being wealthy and famous. Yet famous and wealthy people are not immune to misery, depression and even suicide. So, therefore, gaining wealth and fame without happiness is not reaching the desired destination.

Being in a state or condition that you are not able to possess or enjoy to some extent the basic emotional desires of peace, joy, hope, and love can hardly be considered success because it is a destination or aim that we all have.

Generally, success involves more than the material. It will include our emotional/spiritual and physical health. What some may consider emotional health may be considered by some as spiritual health. The two are intertwined.

Of course, the greatest news is that those desires of peace, joy, hope, and love are attainable by anyone who commits their life to God.

We also need to recognize that even though success contains an element of satisfaction, it is not this utopia where we will feel like we have arrived with no further destination.

This can be another misconception that success is really only counted up at the end of our life once the scorecard is complete, and we have nothing else to do but sit on the beach or play golf.

For many of us, this does not sound all that exciting. Why is that?

God created us to be fruitful and to do things. So, naturally, we have this desire placed in us to accomplish things, to create, serve and build. It is mandated by the Master Builder, so, of course, it gives us great pleasure to do so.

So, success can be experienced by us in varying degrees every year, every week and even each day.

Success is not only arriving at a destination but being on the right route.

Following is a quote from Tim Keller's book Counterfeit Gods where he explains that, <u>Success, defined as being the master of your own destiny</u>, has become a cultural idol.

More than other idols, personal success and achievement lead to a sense that we ourselves are God. . . . To be the very best at what you do, to be at the top of the heap, means no one is like you. You are supreme.

So how do we define success from a biblical viewpoint? God gives us some perspective on how he views success with the parable of the talents beginning in Matthew 25:14

14 "For the kingdom of heaven is like a man traveling to a far country, who called his own servants and delivered his goods to them. 15 And to one he gave five talents, to another two, and to another one, to each according to his own ability; and immediately he went on a journey.16 Then he who had received the five talents went and traded with them, and made another five talents. 17 And likewise he who had received two gained two more also. 18 But he who had received one went and dug in the ground, and hid his lord's money. 19 After a long time the lord of those servants came and settled accounts with them.

20 "So he who had received five talents came and brought five other talents, saying, 'Lord, you delivered to me five talents; look, I have gained five more talents besides them.' 21 His lord said to him, 'Well done, good and faithful servant; you were faithful over a few things, I will make you ruler over many things. Enter into the joy of your lord.'22 He also who had received two talents came and said, 'Lord, you delivered to me two talents; look, I have gained two more talents besides them.' 23 His lord said to him, 'Well done, good and faithful servant; you have been faithful over a few things, I will make you ruler over many things. Enter into the joy of your lord.'

24 "Then he who had received the one talent came and said, 'Lord, I knew you to be a hard man, reaping where you have not sown, and gathering where you have not scattered seed. 25 And I was afraid, and went and hid your talent in the ground. Look, there you have what is yours.'

26 "But his lord answered and said to him, 'You wicked and lazy servant, you knew that I reap where I have not sown, and gather where I have not scattered seed. 27 So you ought to have deposited my money with the bankers, and at my coming I would have received back my own with interest. (NKJV)

It is quite clear in verse 15 that one, we are accountable, and, two, we have not all been given the same abilities.

It is also clear that we are only held accountable to the ratio of our abilities, that we are not of lesser value if we have lesser abilities. Even the most handicapped person who may have very limited opportunities in life can still experience more success than a very talented person who misses his calling.

Our success is dependent on what we do with what we are given. And what we are given is sufficient for our calling.

I would venture to say that there is a universal standard for success even though it does contain a variable.

Success is measured by how well we prosper our master's kingdom.

The variable in this is who we have made our master.

The world has generally made self the master. That is who the world serves.

For the Christian, it is God whom we seek to prosper. We are accountable to use what we have been given to prosper His kingdom. God does want us to be successful.

First things first, how can we know we have the right master? Is being viewed as successful the most important thing to us? What is most important?

Here are two more quotes from Tim Keller's book Counterfeit Gods:

A counterfeit god (idol) is anything so central and essential to your life that, should you lose it, your life would feel hardly worth living.

If anything becomes more fundamental than God to your happiness, meaning in life and identity, then it is an idol.

These become great qualifiers for us to use to evaluate the things in our life.

It is easy for us to fall into idolatry because just like the age of the Romans, who had a god for everything, anything can be a god to us.

Where we find our highest value is ultimately what will be our master.

I can tell you what I believe and even believe that I believe it, but it is only knowledge unless I'm living it. What I live I truly believe.

This doesn't mean that everything that has value is automatically an idol to us.

It is also very clear that we are to work and that it will take work to accomplish success. God used the terms wicked and lazy to describe the one that buried his talent.

This word talent can refer to various things, but the word that was used in the bible was a sum of money and presumably quite a large sum of money. But, I believe this includes all that God gives to us and especially what we today call our natural talents.

Regarding these talents that we sometimes refer to as natural, we need to be careful not to believe the flip side of the lie, "we can be anything we want to be" and start thinking that we can't do anything!

This is just as big of a lie, and we at times like to take comfort in our laziness by saying, "oh, we could never do that" whenever we encounter a highly developed talent such as a great artist, musician, engineer or even athlete. Greatness never just happened.

Greatness is the result of diligent practice and training.

Now, we might think that pursuing greatness or being the best we can be will only lead to pride. It is true, great accomplishments can lead to pride if we are wanting success for that other master "self" or using the biblical term "our flesh". But if we see ourselves as stewards of the gifts that we have been given, then the development of our craft and the training and pursuit of success can be one of the highest forms of worship if it is dedicated to the God that gave it to us in the first place.

Developing your God-given talent is a true act of worship.

THE MINDSET OF SUCCESS

I do not endorse the humanist philosophy of the "Health and Wealth" or "Prosperity" gospel, which is a false gospel, and such associated ideas that we hold the power to wealth and healing through positive thinking and speaking. This is not a biblical principle.

There are many biblical principles, though, that does speak to what our mindset should be. We are to take every thought captive and know that all power has been given to the Lord our Savior, Jesus Christ.

We are to think on those things that are true, honorable, just, pure, lovely and commendable, things that are of excellence and worthy of praise.

The practice of these principles will create a mindset that is conducive to success. Along with these, there are a few other fundamental attitudes or disciplines that are essential for this mindset.

2 Cor 4 For the weapons of our warfare are not carnal but mighty in God for pulling down strongholds, 5 casting down arguments and every high thing that exalts itself against the knowledge of God, bringing every thought into captivity to the obedience of Christ

THANKFULNESS

It is most difficult to complain or even worry when we are truly thankful. I believe that thankfulness is perhaps the first and most crucial attitude to cultivate and own.

If we see the later part of Romans 1 being a progression of sin, then the first step to falling into sin is to not be thankful.

Romans 1:21 because, although they knew God, they did not glorify Him as God, nor were thankful, but became futile in their thoughts, and their foolish hearts were darkened.

FORGIVENESS

Forgiveness is not only a biblical commandment, it is one of the most powerful tools that the bible gives us. Forgiveness allows us to step out of those chains that others will sometimes attempt to put on us.

When we choose to not forgive those that do wrong to us, we are giving them a license to hold a certain amount of control over us. Unforgiveness can have a crippling effect on us. We soon start reacting out of this, and when we are hurt, we will tend to hurt others.

This will not only hinder our success but will give way to bitterness. Bitterness will rob you of all joy.

Romans 12:19 Beloved, do not avenge yourselves, but rather give place to wrath; for it is written, "Vengeance is Mine, I will repay," says the Lord.

CHARITY

I like the term charity for this because not only is it the old English word for love, but it also is the modern word for helping those in need.

If we understand the proper mindset of stewardship,

that everything we have is not really ours but has been given to us to manage, and that the only thing we really get to keep is that which we give away, out of love for our fellow man and not because we have to, then we are equipped for true success.

The world would see wealth as one of the great hallmarks of success. Yet, we see supposedly successful people, or at least wealthy people, commit suicide amidst great depression. Clearly, wealth is not the core of success.

Providing help where needed is a core trait of success.

Matthew 25:34 Then the King will say to those on his right, 'Come, you who are blessed by my Father, inherit the kingdom prepared for you from the foundation of the world. 35 For I was hungry and you gave me food, I was thirsty and you gave me drink, I was a stranger and you welcomed me, 36 I was naked and you clothed me, I was sick and you visited me, I was in prison and you came to me.' ESV

Malachi 3:10 Bring all the tithes into the storehouse, That there may be food in My house, And try Me now in this," Says the Lord of hosts, "If I will not open for you the windows of heaven And pour out for you such blessing that there will not be room enough to receive it.

OPPORTUNITIES THAT BITE

Failed attempts are anything but fun. It's one of the things that hold us back from trying in the first place. We think of failure as being shameful. What if it doesn't work? What will others think of me? We fear failure, and yet, it is one of the best things that can come along because in all reality if we didn't experience failures at times, we would have no need to be innovative.

The fear of failure may quite well be the single biggest detriment to ingenuity.

Without failure, there would be no need for innovation.

Failures and trials are simply opportunities that are trying to get our attention and is why they have to bite a little so we pay attention. It's an opportunity banging on your leg like an impatient child trying to get your attention to say "here is a problem that needs a solution!" Fix me please!

Our failures hold the keys to our greatest success

It's those little failures, or rather those opportunities that bite, that give us the motivation and inspiration to create a solution so we don't have to endure that again! Keep your eyes peeled for those pesky little problems because they just might be your next big success!

WINNERS WILL LOSE

No one likes to lose.

The fact remains, however. We will have losses.

The only way we won't have a loss is if we never try anything, and not trying is the worst kind of losing.

We will lose a sale. We will lose clients. We may have to cut our losses on a project that failed. We may lose money on a new product we tried to sell or develop.

The most successful winners know how to handle failures.

They know when to try again and how to persevere and to not give up on a goal.

A very common story is that of Edison's reply when he

was asked if he wasn't discouraged after he had failed over a hundred times in his attempts to create an electric light bulb. His reply was "I now know more than a hundred ways that it doesn't work". He saw it as a process of elimination.

This is where we take a SMART goal and make it smartER. We utilize the Evaluation and Reward. Every project, whether successful or not, should be evaluated against the reward or the benefits of the results. This is called risk management.

Did the project produce the appropriate dividends for the effort that it required?

Sometimes doing a good thing is bad when it is not the best thing.

Even good things take resources that could be spent on better things. Does the project fit your mission statement? Is it worth the risks for the results?

Properly evaluating a loss is the key to your next success.

Our tendency is to quickly launch into something else to try to make up for lost ground, but if a loss is not properly evaluated and understood why it was lost or why it wasn't a good fit for the company, it will very likely result in duplicating that same loss.

When a client is lost, is the proper evaluation done on why that loss occurred? Was it a failure in the service? Were we trying to provide something that wasn't a good fit for the company?

Not every client will be a good fit for you. Recognizing what you do well and knowing who your target client is can help eliminate losing them later or wasting efforts that could have been directed at your best clients.

Properly parsing your losses is that bumpy road that leads to success.

CHAPTER 8

CONTROLLING CHAOS

 *atthew 6:33 But seek first the kingdom of God and His righteousness, and all these things shall be added to you. NKJV*

PERSONAL WELLNESS

Building and running a small business can be most rewarding when things are good. But the reality is that it is usually quite stressful and a lot of work. It is important that we maintain ourselves. It's not only the most elaborate part but the most valuable part of our business.

When we produce a product or provide a service, we can only do what we are equipped for. Having the right tools and keeping our equipment in good shape and running smoothly is a high priority, and generally, we will have a maintenance program in place to prevent any downtime. We shouldn't treat our most valuable asset with any less care.

In physics, the second law of thermodynamics states that a closed system that has no additional energy input will degenerate into chaos. This applies to both business and our personal wellbeing. We cannot expect to continually manage, mentor, minister and create without refueling ourselves.

The following wellness assessment wheel, Fig. 9.1, depicts a regular life assessment wheel that many people use in slight variations. You rate each part of your life on a scale from one to ten and shade in each related section. This is helpful in having a visual reference on how balanced you think your life is and help you set goals in the areas you want to improve.

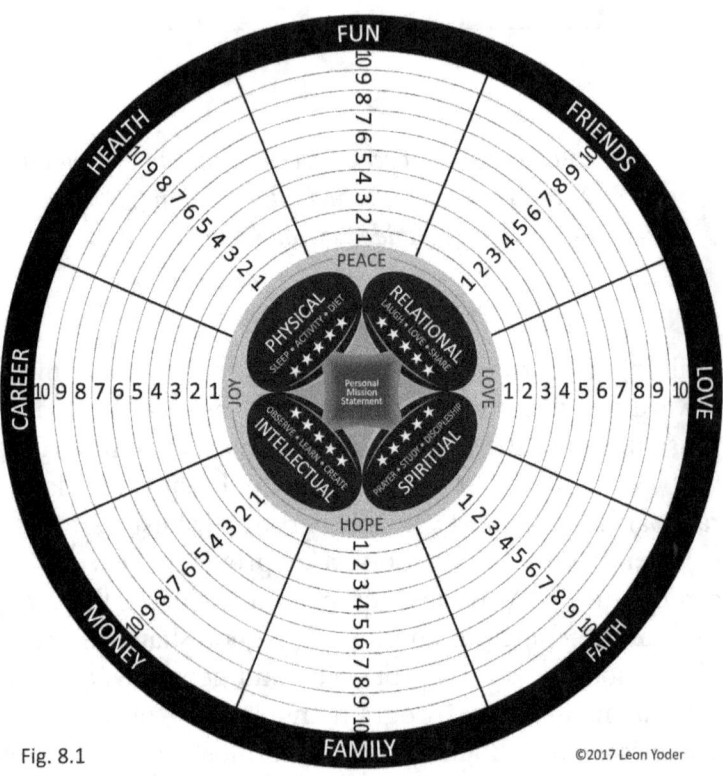

Fig. 8.1   ©2017 Leon Yoder

This wheel is different because of the center hub. This is a personal wellness hub and is shown separately in Fig. 9.2. I do not believe that we will be effective in the extended areas of our life if we are not constantly filling these four areas of our personal life.

PERSONAL MISSION STATEMENT

In the center of this personal wellness hub is a personal mission statement. It is surprising the focus and motivation that it can provide to establish a core statement like this. The key to a personal mission statement is to make sure it is concise enough and not so large and vague that it doesn't apply to daily life. Imagine that tomorrow is the last day of your life, and as you look back over your life, you ask yourself what legacy you want to leave behind.

We all want our life to have significance, and even if people don't remember us, we can affect many generations after us by what we do. People will think that fame is significance, but that is not true. You can be very famous and not have any real significant impact on people. This is an opportunity to still do what you can't do at the end of your life, to focus on how you will impact those around you. Remember that your business is simply a tool to help you accomplish your life goals.

Your mission statement might be a few sentences long but the shorter the better.

A good way to start is to write a sentence or two relating to the different people in your life. For example, "As a parent, I want to... As a spouse, I want to... As a business owner, I want to..." You can also focus on creating a sentence from each of the four basic categories below. Then work on condensing it into a shorter statement. Sometimes people get stuck writing a statement because they are afraid it will feel outdated in a few years when they get a little older and their perspective changes. Don't worry, it's not written in stone. You can change this statement whenever you need to throughout your life. As you go through different stages of life you may sense your purpose changing. It's your statement, so you can change it if and when you want to. My personal statement is; "To bring a value, above that which is required, to every relationship I encounter." Do I always accomplish this? No, but it does provide an inspiration and a daily goal.

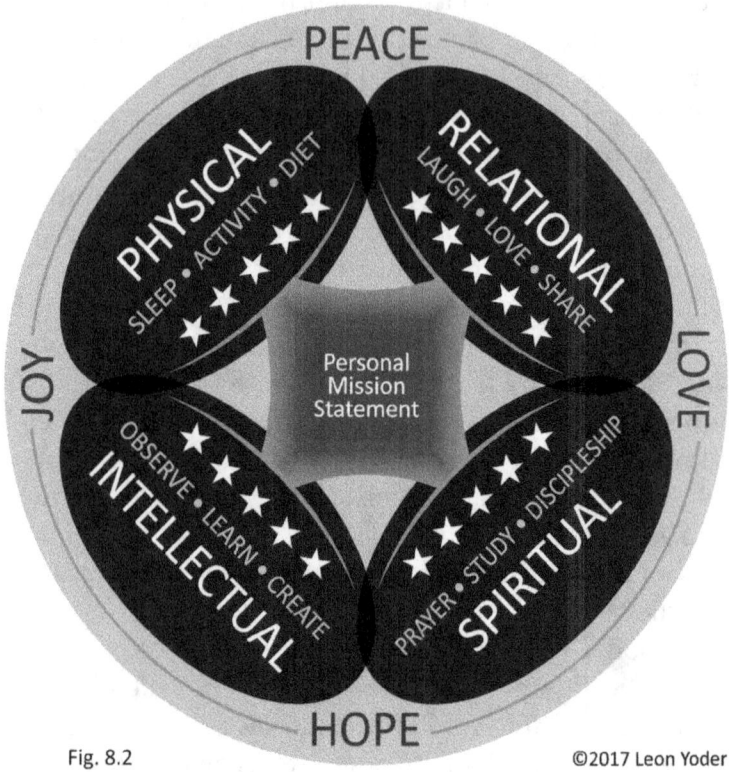

Fig. 8.2   ©2017 Leon Yoder

FOUR PERSONAL RESOURCES

I sometimes refer to the four primary areas as personal buckets because we have to keep filling them, but unlike a regular bucket, you cannot fill these fast. A slow steady stream or even a drip will do more than an occasional downpour. You can rate these areas with one to five stars, and as you make goals, I recommend you only make one goal in each area and continue for a month until it becomes a regular practice.

I have found that each of these areas affects the others. If we are rested and physically feeling well, we will also respond better to others in our relationships and feel more creative. It is also more difficult to maintain prayer and study if we aren't well rested.

The intellectual area can be stimulated in many ways. I have found doing something creative like painting can stimulate ideas in a completely different realm. I have done free-hand pinstriping since I was a young man, and I still do some pinstriping on horse-drawn vehicles. I find that this is some of my most creative time. The same can be accomplished with many other hobbies and activities such as taking a walk through the woods or visiting a museum. These activities may inspire an idea for a new product or a new procedure for your production process or something completely unrelated to what you are doing.

Of course, reading, itself, is one of the most valuable ways of renewing your intellectual resources.

The outer circle encompasses four elements that I believe are desired by every person, and if one of these is missing, it will hinder the sense of fulfillment in our lives. I'm obviously writing from a Christian perspective, and these four, love, peace, joy and hope, are fundamental things in the Christian life, although there are still times that some of these seem to elude us.

TIME MANAGEMENT OR PERSONAL PRODUCTIVITY

There are seemingly endless books and articles written on time management, which seems like such a misnomer because time really cannot be managed. We can manage our actions and our productivity within a time frame, but we cannot slow it down, defer it, store it up or manage it whatsoever. We each have 24 hours each day, no more and no less, and it comes and goes in consistently perfect time. So we are stuck with just trying to manage our actions and improve our productivity as we utilize that time.

MYTHS

Multitasking

There are certain myths about productivity that have been proven wrong but are still being used. One of these is multi-tasking. It is common to hear multitasking being referred to as a great ability. Numerous studies have proven that multitasking is not efficient. Our brain does not process tasks simultaneously but in sequence. Every time a switch is made from one task to another, the efficiency goes down. Add multiple tasks to the mix, and the efficiencies are decreased even more. One study showed as much as a 20% loss in efficiency for each task that was added. For example, multitasking three tasks would create a 40% loss (wasted time) in the overall time it takes to complete all three projects.

Overtime

This one I'm as guilty of as anyone, but studies show that overtime is not productive. Personal productivity peaks just short of forty hours. Even if the work is not physical, the ability to make clear and concise decisions will decline rapidly after an eight hour period.

We have probably all been part of a late week rally where everyone is pulled in to finish a major project, and a great sense of accomplishment is shared as everyone works late to complete it. This has to be done at times, but it should be seen as a failure and not a success because it causes great inefficiencies working in this manner. First, you have people doing work that they generally don't do, so they will not be as efficient because of their lack in both training and practice. Plus, if the labor hours are going over 40 hours, overtime applies, and this is a cost that directly increases operating costs and lowers profitability.

> Overtime is not a sign of commitment. It is a sign of failure. -Jeff Sutherland

Larger Teams

Another study by Fred Brooks found that adding manpower to a software project that is running late will only make the project later. The reason is that larger teams take more effort than those with 5 or fewer people. One of the primary factors is the number of communication channels required. With each additional team member, the number of communications to track increases exponentially. Therefore more and more effort has to be devoted to just tracking the information.

FROM SELF-EMPLOYMENT TO AN ENTREPRENEUR

As a business grows through the different phases, it is probably the chaotic factor that pushes us into new stages where we finally delegate more things to staff simply because of necessity. The self-employed and entrepreneurial mindsets are two distinct mindsets that separate small business. The self-employed is usually the technician that is still trying to do the work in the business, and the entrepreneur has the mindset of developing the business and delegating everything he can. This is the first and probably the most important step in taking control of the chaos. You are limiting the growth of your organization if you do not learn the art of delegation.

The lack of delegation was a problem for me. Looking back it was one of my biggest regrets that I did not do more of it earlier. One of the areas that I was not good at was scheduling. I did have an assistant that was very good at what she did and would have excelled at handling the schedule if I had delegated that responsibility to her. Even though I was the owner and at one time did most of the designing along with finalizing the sale, I could have and should have passed off the job to her after I closed the sale to have her schedule the work. The company could have capitalized on her talents and we would have had much better customer service.

Understanding the personalities and abilities of your team is crucial in knowing what to delegate to whom. A written job description that clearly defines their role and not only the responsibility but also the authority that they have to do specific things is very important.

CONTROLLING CHAOS

One of the biggest challenges today is to handle the immense amount of information that bombards us every day. From emails and phone calls to even texts and notes from meetings and to keep all that data accessible and usable is an art in itself. In addition to all that information, are the interruptions that are created from the flow of that data. It doesn't just show up in a nice manila folder but arrives in bits and pieces throughout the day intent on destroying whatever productivity that you might be enjoying for a brief moment. If you do not choose how to control it, it will try to control you.

One of the first steps in taking charge of your day is to identify the most productive times of your day. Using a red, orange, and yellow marker or highlighter and on a printed calendar, preferably a one-week planner page, mark along the side the hours that are your highest energy hours. These peak productivity areas should be reserved for your most intense tasks. Use the orange marker to select the less productive times and the yellow to mark the lowest energy time slots that you can use for research, checking email etc. This will assist in planning the next step of time blocking.

Time blocking is simply blocking out certain parts of your day for certain types of tasks. One of the most disruptive ways of working is to check email every 15 or 20 minutes or even worse have a popup notify you whenever a text or email shows up. We live in a world where instant gratification is king and it has created some very bad habits for us, thinking we have to reply instantly to every text and email that shows up. Of course, there is also the error on the other end of not getting to emails in a timely manner.

To best utilize these blocks of time you can then list a few of your top projects for the week and then break down those projects into 20-25 minute subtasks that you can prioritize by placing the most intense or difficult tasks within the red zone and spreading the less intense tasks into the orange and yellow zones. Putting time frames into the task can help in keeping a slight grip on the reality of what you can actually accomplish. Planning on 20-25 minute tasks also allow for a 5-minute break every half hour. Taking breaks is crucial, especially if you are sitting at a desk most of the day. The short cycles also help the focus but the higher focus can also cause fatigue making the short breaks even more important. A

Pomodoro timer or timer app is helpful reminding you to take those breaks. The Pomodoro technique is a method developed by Francesco Cirillo in the late 1980's that uses four 25 minute tasks with 3-5 minute breaks and then a 10-15 minute break after the fourth task. Breaking projects down into these smaller segments are very useful in staying on track and keeping a sense of the progress that is being made.

Prioritizing the right things is sometimes difficult. The 80/20 rule or the Pareto Principle as it formally referred to applies to time management as well. Twenty percent of our work will produce eighty percent of the value. As we select the tasks for the day and we begin selecting our tasks based on value rather than urgency we will ultimately create more value by the end of the day. The value might be in what part of our work is billable or it might be the tasks that contribute to more value because it will assist a complete team of people to be productive on a high-value project.

David Allen of Getting Things Done fame explains the technique of doing a brain dump. This can be quite helpful in clearing a desk and your mind of clutter. We think that remembering a simple little thing is no big deal, but there is value in purging all the little notes in your brain onto paper. Writing everything down and sorting these notes into a tickler file for reminders is very helpful in being able to work unhindered and undistracted by those random thoughts of, "did I follow up with Bill on his question," or that "oh I can't forget to call Joe", and the list goes on.

A tickler file is a simple folder with 31 tabs, one for each day of the month and then have a file with a folder for each month. You sort your paper notes into those things you have to do today and everything else gets put into the tabbed folder on the day you want to be reminded and if it's beyond a month out you put it into that corresponding month folder. At the first of each month, you distribute the notes of that folder into your daily tabs. The key is you put a mark on the note each time you move it and once it has three marks you can't move it again. You have to either do it or pitch it. If you use a digital calendar, you can simply put a reminder directly into the all day part of your calendar for a specific followup you want to do that day. With many of the digital apps, you can also set a reminder for the tasks on your to-do lists.

Sometimes we have to do what we gotta do to outsmart ourselves to overcome our weaker tendencies.

UNFINISHED BUSINESS

In my early twenties, I was working with a business associate who was interested in purchasing a local business. He asked me to go meet with the business owner and do the preliminary scouting.

I was familiar with the industry that the business was in and was skeptical that there would be big enough margins in this business to justify the purchase.

After meeting with the owner and getting the financial report, the numbers confirmed what I feared was true.

My associate would hardly believe that the report was accurate. He could not believe that a business could grow to that size on those margins.

He, himself, met with the owner to review the financials in more detail and to see if there was any trace of unreported income. There wasn't.

It was a business that did some manufacturing, but a majority of the business was selling wholesale parts. So, there was a huge inventory built up over many years.

The business was able to provide a meager income for the business owner that was directly involved in the business. However, the amount of investment that was required just to purchase the inventory was too large for the return that could be made on the profit margins, so it simply was not a feasible investment.

This is one of the two most common reasons why a small business cannot be sold. It has grown too large for the amount of profit that it can produce. It simply isn't feasible for a new business owner to borrow the money and be able to pay back the loan plus make a living wage.

The second reason is probably the most common reason.

This is where a business is so dependent on the day-to-day involvement of the owner that the business would cease to exist if the owner were to step away.

Another element to this is that, when a business owner has such a crucial role in the daily operations, it will usually mean that he is also the primary interaction with the clients, and there will be a large risk of losing clients when the ownership changes.

This is the dilemma of an unfinished business-a business that was started but never completed with the tools and systems to run on its own.

So how do you prevent this? How do you complete a business?

To complete a business is to have the business structured in such a manner that the owner is able to step away, at least for a short period of time, and the business is able to continue without him.

This requires a business to establish written systems and procedures for every aspect of the business, from an organizational chart for every position in the business to complete job descriptions for every job that has to be done, everything from answering the telephone to closing the office, from every step of production to the billing and collections process.

The ideal approach is to pretend you will be franchising your business, knowing that you will have to provide a 3-ring binder that details every step of operating your business.

Yes, it is a lot of work. But the freedom it brings to the owner of a business is unparalleled.

Hopefully, this book will have provided the inspiration to take those steps and build a business that serves you versus you being enslaved to it. Can you do it all on your own? No. It takes a team, so choose carefully. Different companies will face different problems, and it's not unusual for companies and individuals to hit plateaus that they can't break through. There are many specialists available that can help. But again, choose carefully. Make sure the vision and values are the same as yours.

This brings us to our next section. The role of a business coach.

THE BENEFITS OF A COACH

The reason I first began developing systems for my business many years ago was because of a business coach.

I was convinced that my business was too unique to utilize systems effectively. To an extent, it was unique, as is almost every small business. We were designing and building custom signs and graphics, and there was seemingly nothing standard from one job to the next.

However, I decided that if I could build systems for this kind of business, then I knew systems would work for any business out there.

Systems allowed me to become involved in other business opportunities that would not have been possible if I would have had to maintain a day-to-day involvement. If not only allowed me to eventually sell the business, but it also kept me from getting burned out. I was able to enjoy the business from a whole other perspective.

I found over the years of working with new business start-ups that I really enjoyed helping my clients establish new logos and assist with rebranding and in their overall marketing efforts.

So when I was offered the opportunity to become a business coach, I knew this was where my passion was, not only helping small businesses with their marketing but to help them develop systems and experience a new freedom in owning a small business.

I was excited about this new opportunity until about the next day.

I began having doubts.

Who do I think I am that I can coach businessmen that probably have a larger company than I ever did? They probably have experience in areas that I don't.

I pondered this for some time, and then, I began to see another perspective of a coach.

I had to think of Michael Jordan and other great athletes who were capable of executing plays that no coach could ever do. Yet even the greatest athletes have a coach.

Jordan's coach, Mike Jackson, was not capable of doing the plays that he trained his players to do.

So could Jordan have taken the Chicago Bulls to multiple championships without a coach?

I am sure they would have experienced some success but hardly to the extent that they did with Coach Mike Jackson.

A coach is able to bring a perspective to the game that the players cannot.

This is where I became excited again about coaching because of the possibility of assisting other teams to greater things than what I could ever accomplish on my own, to be able to assist other leaders and managers in taking them to their own championships.

THE OUTSIDE ADVANTAGE

Whenever you propose major changes in a company and where any number of employees are involved, there will be resistance. Some people love change, but many will resist it, especially when those changes appear to have the potential to make an individual look bad.

The very concept of implementing change to improve something gives the connotation that someone isn't doing their job. This can be a strong negative influence on employees and cause them to try to undermine the whole process.

When anyone within the line of management suggests change, the motives are immediately questioned.

So is this person trying to go over my head? How will this affect me and my job security?.

The first advantage that an outside coach or consultant can have is to assist in bringing the team together without bias and the only agenda being the betterment of a company. A good consultant can help facilitate this.

The second advantage is the objectivity that an outsider can bring. It is amazing how quickly you will accept certain procedures as being normal when you are involved with the daily work of a company and no longer question the steps that are being taken to accomplish certain tasks. It's just the way something is done.

Of course, a consultant or coach will bring expertise and training that are focused on troubleshooting company growth issues and help navigate through those.

CHOOSING THE RIGHT COACH

When is the right time or stage in business that is most appropriate to hire a coach?

How do you choose the right coach?

Having a business coach will have a big effect on your company, which can be either good or bad.

So how can you be sure that you have made the right choice?

Here are a few things to consider.

- Experience. What is the experience of the coach in both owning and operating a small business as well as the coaching profession?

- Reputation. The coach should, of course, be reputable. Are there testimonies available from other people that the coach has worked with?

- Values. Does the coach hold the same values? It is important to be equally yoked in this area.

- Vision. Does the coach understand your vision and the goals that you have both personally and as a business?

- Availability. Is the coach available and accessible for those times you need some help on an unexpected matter

- ◦ Suitable Plan. Last but definitely not least, is the plan suitable for you? Is the plan paced appropriately for the time that you will be able to invest?

- ◦ Resources. Do you have the time and resources to make the changes that will be required? You will probably need to delegate some of your current tasks, and you may need assistance to document some of the systems if you don't want to do all that yourself.

Recognize that it is not a bad thing if either you or the coach feel that one of you is not a good fit for the other.

Prepare to be committed to spending some time in working on your business. You might think you don't have time, but you don't have time not to.

Remember, we tend to have our focus on getting to the destination, but God often seems more concerned about the journey. It's the preparation for something greater, so embrace the journey!